Praise for *Remarkable*

"Brady is practical and inspiring. I think you'll find yourself wanting this remarkable life with God!"

—John Eldredge, president, Ransomed Heart

"As a mom of six with a busy corporate life, I expected to skim this book for a thought or two. Instead, I simply could not put it down. It strikes at such a deep desire for a remarkable life, and offers real-life, practical ideas for small shifts with big dividends. This rich content is written for the NOW challenges we face as parents, spouses, and leaders. I will definitely be borrowing these truths for those I lead."

—Lynette Lewis, TEDx speaker, pastor's wife, and NYC-based author of *Climbing the Ladder in Stilettos*

"Brady Boyd is my pastor and I get to sit under his teaching and leadership each week. He walks with Jesus so intimately and sees culture so clearly, his teaching consistently connects God's solutions to the real needs of life without compromising love . . . ever. *Remarkable* is a winsome guide for any Jesus follower wanting to live life to the full in a world that doesn't always follow Jesus.

Santiago "Jimmy" Mellado, president and CEO, Compassion International

"The way we treat those who are not like us, the way we model grace, the way we handle our sexuality, the way we think about marriage and family, the way we steward influence and power—all of it and more testifies to the kingdom we belong to and makes us a 'remarkable' people indeed. Read this book carefully. Digest its message. And then go and live it. The world needs it."

—Andrew Arndt, associate and teaching pastor, New Life Friday Night

"When faced with the daunting cultural, moral, and social challenges of the modern world, most Christians will either fight, retreat, or surrender. But Brady Boyd offers a fourth option, gleaned from the life and example of the apostle Paul and steeped in the truth of Scripture. Now, I may not embrace every viewpoint Brady expresses in his new book, but I do know this: *Remarkable* will help you more effectively and graciously demonstrate Christ's love to those around you—especially those with whom you disagree."

—Jim Daly, president, Focus on the Family

"If you are ready to stand out, make a difference, and live a remarkable life then this is the book for you. My friend, Brady Boyd, shows us the way to walk through today's culture with faith, hope, and love. With every page he reminds us that in a world full of options Jesus is still the only way to a truly remarkable life."

—John Stickl, lead pastor, Valley Creek Church, and author of *Follow the Cloud*

"Evangelism is about LOVE, pure and simple. Jesus' life was a story of His love for the worst, the lowest, the down-and-out. In this "remarkable" book, Brady Boyd outlines a pattern, a mosaic of love stories where Jesus Christ has done it again . . . through us. Become the hands, feet, and kindness of Christ extended to a desperate world. His reward is for those who DO!

—Larry Stockstill, executive director of the Surge Project

"*Remarkable* is a deeply encouraging book that brings with it a wind of encouragement for the times in which we live. Brady Boyd has given us another book that is rich in Scripture, Spirit empowered, and culturally in tune. I'll be sharing this book with our leaders for sure!

—Ron Lewis, founding pastor and overseer, King's Park International Church, and senior pastor, Every Nation NYC

"Pastor Brady's timely message in *Remarkable* will most likely encourage some and hit others hard, just like Jesus did! But we have to learn to love others right where they are, before they know Jesus, and my good friend shows you some practical ways to do that without feeling like you're compromising your faith or your integrity.

—Rick Bezet, lead pastor, New Life Church of Arkansas, and author of *Be Real* and *Real Love in an Angry World*

"We live in a complicated world. Pastor Brady Boyd shows how the wisdom of Scripture still applies, from the church to the office to the family and beyond."

—Jimmy Evans, senior pastor, Gateway Church

remarkable

LIVING A *FAITH* WORTH *TALKING* ABOUT

BRADY BOYD

HOWARD BOOKS

ATRIA

NEW YORK LONDON TORONTO SYDNEY NEW DELHI

An Imprint of Simon & Schuster, Inc.
1230 Avenue of the Americas
New York, NY 10020

Published in association with The Bindery Agency, www.TheBinderyAgency.com

First Howard Books/Atria Paperback edition August 2020

For information about special discounts for bulk purchases, please contact Simon & Schuster Special Sales at 1-866-506-1949 or business@simonandschuster.com.

The Simon & Schuster Speakers Bureau can bring authors to your live event. For more information or to book an event, contact the Simon & Schuster Speakers Bureau at 1-866-248-3049 or visit our website at www.simonspeakers.com.

Interior design by Michelle Marchese

Manufactured in the United States of America

1 3 5 7 9 10 8 6 4 2

Library of Congress Cataloging-in-Publication Data

Names: Boyd, Brady, author.
Title: Remarkable : living a faith worth talking about / by Brady Boyd.
Description: First Howard Books hardcover edition. | New York : Howard Books, 2019. | Includes bibliographical references.
Identifiers: LCCN 2019003109 (print) | ISBN 9781982101374 (hardcover : alk paper)
Subjects: LCSH: Christian life—Biblical teaching. | Christianity and culture. | Bible. Corinthians, 1st—Criticism, interpretation, etc.
Classification: LCC BS2675.6.C48 B69 2019 (print) | LCC BS2675.6.C48 (ebook) | DDC 248.4—dc23
LC record available at https://lccn.loc.gov/2019003109
LC ebook record available at https://lccn.loc.gov/2019981383

ISBN 978-1-9821-0137-4
ISBN 978-1-9821-0138-1 (pbk)
ISBN 978-1-9821-0139-8 (ebook)

To all the men, women, pastors, neighbors, colleagues, family members, and friends who have lived remarkable lives in front of me. Your witness spurs me on.

Contents

remarkable

1

Corinth, U.S.A.

What's in a Name?

Drinking beer is easy. Trashing your hotel room is easy.
But being a Christian, that's a tough call.
That's rebellion.

ALICE COOPER

Two thousand years ago—first in Asia, and then in the Roman Empire and throughout Europe—if you wanted to know about someone's life, you simply asked them about their name. For instance, if you were speaking with someone in China who said that his surname was Wang—meaning king—then you'd know that person hailed from a royal line. If you met someone named Li—meaning a follower of Taoism—then you'd know that person was a descendant of that particular religion.

Spreading into Europe, if you happened upon sisters Antonia Major and Antonia Minor, you'd immediately know (a) that they were the daughters of an Antonius and (b) which was the older child. Later, to encounter Joe *Smith* or Sam *Potter* or Ed *Taylor* or Fran *Webster* was to know what these people did for a living: blacksmith, potter, tailor, weaver. During the Middle Ages, resourced people ate fine, white bread, while under-resourced people ate coarse, dark bread, and so to meet someone with the surname Whitebread—or, later, Whitbread—was to know their socioeconomic standing in life.

A man surnamed Andrews was Andrew's son. A man surnamed Stevenson was Steven's son. A man surnamed Richardson was Richard's son. "Atkins" came from "Adkins," which meant Adam's kin. "Dawkins" came from "Davkins," which meant David's kin. "Jenkins" came from "Jankins," which meant Jan's kin.

Julia who lived by the village green was dubbed Julia Greene.

Malik who lived by the holly trees was dubbed Malik Hollis.

Louis who lived in the town's longest valley was dubbed Louis Longbottom.

Robert who lived by the town's walls was dubbed Robert Walls.

If a person was arrogant, he might be surnamed Prince.

If a person was strong, she might be surnamed Armstrong.

If a person was surnamed Swift, guess how he walked?

If a person was surnamed Makepeace, you automatically knew how she conducted herself on the heels of a misunderstanding.

There were the Shorts and the Smarts, the Longfellows and the Youngs, the Blunts (blondes) and the Reids (redheads), but—regardless of the specific designation—one thing was certain: a person's name told you much about him or her. A person's name revealed *who they were.*

More than two thousand years ago, in a town called Antioch, people who followed Jesus, people "of the Way," were given a special name. "Christians," they were called (from the Koine Greek word *Christos*)—those who were following the teachings of Christ. In Acts 11:26 (KJV), after Paul encountered Jesus and showed up in Antioch to disciple believers there, the designation was introduced: "The disciples were called Christians first in Antioch."

Later, when the apostle Paul is pleading with Herod Agrippa to come to Jesus and surrender his life, the king interrupts him, asking, "Do you think you can persuade me to become a Christian so quickly?" (Acts 26:28). Then, on the subject of suffering for the gospel, the apostle Peter reminds us that "it is no shame to suffer for being a Christian" (1 Peter 4:16).

To be known as Christian was a meaningful thing. Whatever else was true about you—where you grew up or where you lived, whose son you were or else whose father, whether you were tall or bald or brilliant or old—this was the *truest* thing, this name that said, "I am not attached to the mission and values of Rome but rather the mission and values of Jesus Christ."

Throughout history, God has looked for a group of people who would give themselves wholeheartedly to the idea of radically following him. He has longed for a people who would push aside all other preferences and priorities for the sake of knowing and loving him. "The eyes of the LORD search the whole earth," 2 Chronicles 16:9 tells us, "in order to strengthen those whose hearts are fully committed to him."

This divine strengthening was reserved for believers.

It was reserved for those *serious* about following him.

It was reserved for those who answered joyfully to "Christian."

It was reserved for those whose hearts were fully his.

What God has been searching for since the beginning of time, he searches for still today: a people whose core identity centers on his Son, Jesus; a people remarkably distinguishable from the rest of the world.

A recent study from The Barna Group, a market research firm that statistically scrutinizes the intersection of faith and culture, says that 82 percent of believers polled don't know what the "Great Commission" is. Technically, only 51 percent acknowledge having "never heard of it." But the other 31 percent I lumped into my sum responded either "I'm not sure" or else "I've heard of it, but I can't tell you what it means."[1] No matter how you parse the data, a significant number of people who self-identify as "Christian" and "believer" and "churchgoer" can't quite put their finger on the seminal task that Jesus asked us churchgoers to achieve.

In Matthew 28:18–20, just before he was to leave his disciples and ascend to the presence of his Father, Jesus commissioned his followers with a specific task. "I have been given all authority in heaven and on earth," he says. "Therefore, go and make disciples of all the nations, baptizing them in the name of the Father and the Son and the Holy Spirit. Teach these new disciples to obey all the commands I have given you. And be sure of this: I am with you always, even to the end of the age."

Clearly, Jesus had an expectation of his followers that the faith that saved them and was transforming them wouldn't get stuck with them alone. He dreamed of a reality in which lovers of God would reach out to those struggling to feel loved—both those who know Christ and those who have never encountered him before—and love them as Jesus loves them. In this paradigm, Christ's followers would possess such strength of character and such compassion that they would shine like "bright lights in a world full of crooked and perverse people," as Philippians 2:15 not so subtly puts it. They would be remarkably optimistic. They would be remarkably unoffendable. They would be remarkably forgiving whenever they were wronged. They would be remarkably faithful, remarkably patient, remarkably generous with their resources. They'd be remarkably encouraging, remarkably gracious, and remarkably loving to all.

And perhaps most astounding, by their admirable attitudes and actions *they would compel others to do the same.*

The challenge in achieving this goal, I'm finding, is simply getting out of my own way.

I took my teenage son, Abram, to breakfast at McDonald's one Saturday morning not long ago. We walked up to the counter, placed our order, waited for the nice lady to hand us our tray of saturated fat, and headed off to find a booth. After we sat down and unpacked our bags of food, we realized that the order taker had gotten our order totally wrong. I plunked the food back into the bags, loaded the bags back onto the tray, scooted my way out of the booth, and headed for the counter with a head full of steam.

Here is what my posture was shouting as I approached: *What kind of idiot can't get a simple breakfast order right? Was it the extra Egg McMuffin that threw you off? It's early. I'm irritable. I haven't had coffee. I don't even know* why life is happening *at this hour. Can you try again and this time not screw up?*

Thank goodness there was someone ahead of me in line. I was forced to stand there, errant order in hand, and breathe. By the time I reached the lady, I'd come to my senses again. "Ma'am," I was able to say gently, "I think my son and I got someone else's order by mistake."

This was an especially fortuitous turn of events, given that her reply was "Oh! My mistake. Let me fix that for you. And by the way, *my family and I sure love being part of your church.*"

What is that thing that seems to overtake us between the goal for kind, loving living and our faithfulness to act on that goal? Where is our patience when our spouse forgets to pay a bill? Our forgiveness when someone cuts in front of us in line? Our love when someone gets our breakfast order wrong? Our kindness when a friend says a hurtful word? Our faithfulness when it seems like doing the right thing isn't rewarded like we expect?

Last year, I did a deep dive into the apostle Paul's first recorded letter to the Corinthian church in preparation for a sermon series I wanted to write. I approached my research with curiosity: Was the culture in ancient Greece somehow more conducive to living like Jesus than the one we find ourselves in today? Was it easier to choose righteousness in the year 50 than it is here and now, today? In various places in 1 Corinthians, the apostle exhorted believers to practice what in my estimation are truly amazing feats. A sampling, for our review:

- Live "free from all blame" (1 Corinthians 1:8).
- "Live in harmony with each other" (1 Corinthians 1:10).
- "Let there be no divisions in the church" (1 Corinthians 1:10).
- "Boast only about the LORD" (1 Corinthians 1:31).
- "Don't you realize that all of you together are the temple of God and that the Spirit of God lives in you?" (1 Corinthians 3:16).
- "Stop deceiving yourselves" (1 Corinthians 3:18).
- Stop associating "with anyone who claims to be a believer yet indulges in sexual sin, or is greedy, or worships idols, or is abusive, or is a drunkard, or cheats people" (1 Corinthians 5:11).
- "Run from sexual sin!" (1 Corinthians 6:18).
- "Do not deprive each other [as married couples] of sexual relations, unless you both agree to refrain from sexual

intimacy for a limited time so you can give yourselves more completely to prayer" (1 Corinthians 7:5).

- Practice the type of love that is "patient and kind . . . not jealous or boastful or proud or rude. It does not demand its own way. It is not irritable, . . . keeps no record of being wronged, . . . and does not rejoice about injustice but rejoices whenever the truth wins out. Love never gives up, never loses faith, is always hopeful, and endures through every circumstance" (1 Corinthians 13:4–7).
- "Let love be your highest goal" (1 Corinthians 14:1).

Surely there were no incorrect fast-food breakfast orders in Corinth. It was probably much easier to be holy there.

I was having a conversation this week with an acquaintance of mine who was lamenting all that is wrong in our culture today. "We're losing our way," he said soberly. "It's everywhere . . . teen drug use, mass shootings, vitriol spewed 24/7 on social media, everyone demanding instant gratification, zero attention span, soaring suicide rates . . . Everything is hypersexualized . . . TV commercials sexualize *hamburgers*, for crying out loud . . ." The guy had a point, but—given my immersion in ancient Greece these last twelve months—instead of joining his lament, I said, "You think it's bad now? Compared with Corinth back in Paul's day, we're Main Street at Disney World." (The next time you're at a Disney theme park, toss a piece of trash on the ground. It won't lie there three seconds before a "cast member" swoops in to whisk it out of sight. The place is immaculate—almost sterile.)

To understand the allure of Corinth, we need only to be reminded of its distinct location on the map. Harkening back to middle school geography, you'll recall that an isthmus is a narrow piece of land surrounded on two sides by water. But not all isthmuses are created equal. The sole link between Greece's two highest-profile cities, Athens and Sparta, as well as the central land route for traders needing to trek back and forth between the Aegean and Adriatic Seas, the isthmus of Corinth was a highly coveted piece of land. Eventually, in the nineteenth century, a canal would be dug, but even without it the city boomed. Boats were lugged across giant stones from one side to the other, which meant sailors could avoid the lengthy, often treacherous journey around the Peloponnese. There were plentiful freshwater springs and mounds of fertile soil, making the town highly desirable to prospective residents and merchants alike. And there existed an overemphasis on entertainment, success, and pleasure, which drew the hungry, the greedy, and the lustful . . . in other words, a *whole lot of people* in that day. Corinth was Vegas before Vegas.

Adding to the draw were the biannual Isthmian Games. Second only to the Greece's Olympic Games in popularity, the Isthmian Games were a celebration both of athletic and musical performance, the grand prize being a crown of wild celery. (I hope competitors were in it for more than the prize.) But if you think about the effect of such games on a culture, the licentiousness of Corinth begins to make sense.

In our day, whenever a city is chosen to host, say, the summer Olympics, massive efforts are under way years before the Games arrive. Athletic facilities and a giant main stadium are built or at least repurposed at quite an expense. Hotels, conference centers, and restaurants are erected. Some sort of Olympic Village to house athletes is constructed. Transportation options get sorted out. Sochi spent $51 billion when it hosted the Summer Games, the highest in history, with Beijing a close second at $44 billion. Those outliers help explain why, on average, a city will spend more than $5 billion to host the event, which is still a lot of coin. This kind of resourcing wasn't around in Paul's day, of course, but, relatively speaking, the Games were big. Every two years, people flocked to Corinth to compete and to spectate, and to make money off all those competitors and spectators. The reason Paul himself was thought to have been able to stay in town for as long as he did—eighteen months, by nearly all accounts—was that he was a skilled tentmaker. "Olympic Village" in those days was little more than a glorified tent city. But the carnival vibe of it all . . . imagine such grandiosity, such an adrenaline rush, such a festive atmosphere, not once in a city's lifetime but rather *every twenty-four months.*

The city had been decimated by Roman warriors two hundred years before the apostle Paul's arrival on the scene, during which time the Games were relocated to Sicyon, a neighboring town to the west. In 44 BCE, Corinth was rebuilt by Julius Caesar to be a port town, a key to Grecian trade. It makes sense, then, when Paul arrived in AD 51 that he found all the shine and slickness of new money, which, as most Americans know, can quickly lead to shortsightedness, self-centeredness, and greed.

Spiritually, Corinth was a mixed bag. A melting pot of hundreds of nationalities, both male and female, both enslaved and free, both rich and debilitatingly poor, Corinth seemed unified by the occultic worship of pagan gods. The big deal in the area was the temple of Aphrodite, and to our earlier point about our modern United States reality being like Disney by comparison with Corinth, just imagine having to have sex with a sanctioned "temple prostitute" prior to entering the temple each week to worship.[2] Things here may be bad, my friend, but they aren't *that* bad.

It's telling that people who properly assimilated to life in Corinth, which generally meant taking to sexual escapades that "even pagans do not tolerate" (1 Corinthians 5:1 NIV) and fervent worship of man-made gods—what Paul called drinking "the cup of the Lord and the cup of demons too" (1 Corinthians 10:21 NIV)—were said to have been "Corinthianized" (*korinthiazesthai* in the Greek). And more scandalous to me, the term was worn not as an insult but as an honor badge.[3] The name Corinth means ornament, and you get the feeling, upon reading accounts of chronic misbehavior on the part of many in town, that indeed its value centered on playing the role of superficial adornment rather than that of substance, wholeness, or depth.

Roman slaves who had been set free settled in Corinth to make new lives for themselves. Roman military retirees eager to unplug from a brutal regime and Roman merchants looking to profit from the town's resurgence as a commercial hub came too. Jews who had been banished from Rome established their residence in Corinth, as did some Greeks who were intrigued by all the talk. A million or so in all came to Corinth, among them a handful of believers, little more than a house church—fifty or perhaps one hundred strong. And to them the apostle Paul longed to deliver a message: *You can shine as a remarkable light for Jesus in a culture that has little use for him.*

He could speak those same words to those of us here in our context today . . . You and I can live productively as followers of Jesus in a world that increasingly pays him no mind.

When Paul arrived in Corinth, he stepped into a situation where the body of Christ was being lured by a callous culture to accept cheap substitutes for intimacy with their Creator, to attempt to find fulfillment in pursuits other than him. While the church there was small, the implications of this type of drift were huge. Without some sort of official governing body for the church of Jesus Christ, its survival rested largely on the faithfulness of individual hearts. As we will explore in the pages to come, not much has changed here despite our modern, elaborate "church governance" structures. So much still rides on each faithful human heart.

Regarding his strategy for influencing Corinthians to consider Jesus, Paul was clear: "When I first came to you, dear brothers and sisters," he wrote, "I didn't use lofty words and impressive wisdom to tell you God's secret plan. For I decided that while I was with you I would forget everything except Jesus Christ, the one who was crucified" (1 Corinthians 2:1–2).

In the next verses, Paul admits that he has come to Corinth "in weakness—timid and trembling" (v. 3). This makes sense practically, given that, weeks prior, Paul had been imprisoned and beaten to within inches of his life in Philippi for proclaiming the gospel of Christ. But I believe there's more to the story than that. Despite its Roman influence, Corinth still was a Greek city, and Grecian culture celebrated intellectual prowess. The Greeks *loved* public debate. The great orators of the age would come to Corinth, stand in the public square, and with great expertise defend their views on the big ideas of the time before audiences hundreds and sometimes thousands strong.[4]

Paul hadn't come to do that, even though he certainly could have. He was a Hebrew scholar whose reputation for deftness in debate preceded him, and yet his approach to ministering in Corinth leaned into an entirely different set of skills: "I didn't come to amaze you with my sermon," Paul essentially said. "I didn't come to entertain you in the public square or to win a heated debate. I came to demonstrate the Spirit's power. I came to urge you to let your faith rest not on man's wisdom but on the wisdom that comes from God."

See, while Paul surely was exhausted, frustrated, and in pain following the events in Philippi, his decision to come at things differently was far from an emotional one. Paul knew that this "new life" he spoke of was a foreign concept to those in his midst. This church was young. The believers were *babies*.

And most parents—biological ones and spiritual ones, too—don't read textbooks to babies; they take things down a notch. Here is how Paul explains how and why he has come:

> *Let me now remind you, dear brothers and sisters, of the Good News I preached to you before. You welcomed it then, and you still stand firm in it. It is this Good News that saves you if you continue to believe the message I told you—unless, of course, you believed something that was never true in the first place.*
>
> *I passed on to you what was most important and what had also been passed on to me. Christ died for our sins, just as the Scriptures said. He was buried, and he was raised from the dead on the third day, just as the Scriptures said. He was seen by Peter and then by the Twelve. After that, he was seen by more than 500 of his followers at one time, most of whom are still alive, though some have died. Then he was seen by James and later by all the apostles. Last of all, as though I had been born at the wrong time, I also saw him. For I am the least of all the apostles. In fact, I'm not even worthy to be called an apostle after the way I persecuted God's church.*
>
> *But whatever I am now, it is all because God poured out his special favor on me—and not without results. For I have worked harder than any of the other apostles; yet it was not I but God who was working through me by his grace. So it makes no difference whether I preach or they preach, for we all preach the same message you have already believed [1 Corinthians 15:1–11].*

Paul knew that he could blow endless amounts of time chasing down every manifestation of Corinthian waywardness he saw, or else *he could labor to demonstrate the gospel,* trusting the Spirit to draw tenderized hearts. He chose the latter, which I find instructive for you and me, given the culture we find ourselves in. As you might guess, the people of Corinth were spiritually stubborn. They'd found new freedom, they'd found new resourcefulness, they'd found new opportunities, they'd found new wealth. But Paul knew that even as this new path seemed stimulating and satisfying to Corinthian believers, any path that led to opposition to God was a destructive one. Paul implored them to correct their course.

Thus, the level-setting reminders throughout his letters: *Believers, remember what you've believed,* he pleaded with them. *Christ came. Christ died. Christ rose again from the dead.*

By Christ's power, they could live differently now.

I imagine Paul vying for Corinthian hearts in this way for a full eighteen months and feel exhausted on his behalf. It's tiring to call people to change! A friend asked me why I was so tired one Monday, and I said, "I'm *always* tired on Mondays. Mondays come after Sundays, and on Sundays, I'm putting 100 percent of my energies toward pleading with people to change."

I can speak at a conference or do an hour-long radio interview or lead back-to-back meetings and go home feeling great. But preaching? It's a different beast. When you go up against the gods of this age and ask people to imagine a fresh way of living, a wholly different direct object of their faith, the energy tank gets tapped—and fast. I think of Paul coming off of Philippi and setting foot on this eighteen-month journey to compel Corinth back to Christ, and my heart goes out to him.

This would be an uphill climb if ever there were one. And yet he knew it was a climb that had to be made.

And so he looked into the eyes of those believers at Corinth and said with the compassion of a loving dad to a son that they'd traded something stunning for something sordid. Their pursuit of pleasure had replaced their pursuit of God. They had valued their own ways above the ways of their Father. They now craved chaos instead of peace.

Come back, Paul was imploring them. *Come back to the cross of Christ.*

It wasn't exactly what his listeners wanted to hear. Who wants to talk about a *cross*?

As Christians, we have made the cross palatable. We put flowers around it. We cast it in gold, thread a chain through it, and feel noble about wearing it around our necks. But when Paul was on the earth, the cross represented serious business. This Roman method of execution was so bloody and torturous and awful that you never would have even *alluded* to it in polite company, let alone glorified it. For Paul to preach about a Christ, a Messiah, the Son of God, being crucified was an awful way to start a conversation. Crucifixion was a shameful way to die, and nobody wanted to be reminded that the One they were following, the One they'd devoted their lives to, had been murdered on a Roman cross. This was a culture that celebrated the big, the bold, the successful, the strong, the sensual, the popular, the rich. This image of a poor, weak, vulnerable Jesus being put to death in this manner went against everything they esteemed. Which is precisely why Paul started there. As we'll explore further in chapter 9, the power of entertainment, of sex, and of money gets broken only by the power of the cross.

It is by the power of the cross that believers can live blamelessly.

It is by the power of the cross that unity can have its way.

It is by the power of the cross that churches can operate harmoniously.

It is by the power of the cross that humility can mark a human heart.

It is by the power of the cross that deception gets defeated.

It is by the power of the cross that sin loses its allure.

It is by the power of the cross that true love is practiced.

It is by the power of the cross that cultures see genuine change.

Paul knew that the practical shifts he was asking believers at Corinth to make would happen *only by the power of the cross*, and so, instead of shaking his fist or stomping his feet or disparaging the ones he was hoping to serve, he simply fixed his gaze on the old rugged cross, trusting that there, every wrong would be made right.

2

The Three Responses

Believers in an Unbelieving World

Today, ordinary Americans are being stuffed with garbage.

CARL BERNSTEIN

For more than two thousand years, every Christian community has had to make a choice regarding how they would respond to the culture in which they live. The believers at Corinth made their choice, as did believers living in Ephesus, Jerusalem, and Rome. Believers who lived during the Renaissance had to choose, as did those who lived during the Protestant Reformation. During both the First and Second Great Awakenings, believers had to make their choice, as did believers who lived during the early days of America's founding. Marching down through the ages, during both wartime and peacetime, during the reign of leaders both corrupt and good, during both prosperity and famine, during both spiritual bleakness and growth, believers have had to make their choice: *How will we respond as Christ's followers to the culture in which we live?*

And so, even today, you and I have a choice to make. As we take in the surrounding cultural realities—the darkest of which are marked by rampant self-interest, increased apathy toward the claims of Christ, confusion regarding long-held norms involving marriage and sexuality, and contagious cynicism—what are we to do?

If you've ever read through the book of 1 Corinthians, then you may recall that early in Paul's ministry at Corinth, the apostle acknowledged that his message might read as foolishness to some of the believers gathered there. It is a message of wisdom, he said in 1 Corinthians 2:6, but "not the kind of wisdom that belongs to this world or to the rulers of this world." Interestingly, many Bible scholars believe that Paul was speaking here of the demonic realm, of Satan's influence in the earth, but in fact he was not. So, what *is* Paul referring to? The "wisdom that belongs to the world" is thinking that's apart from God. It is thought, ingenuity, will, and ways that hold no space for God.

To be fair, the Corinthian people had every reason to be impressed with themselves. They had settled in a new land and made a respectable name for themselves. Their growth chart was all up and to the right. . . . Things were looking good, and the town's prosperity had them to thank. Paul didn't come to take any of those gains away from them. Rather, he came to say that there's a wisdom that is greater still.

At its core, Paul's ministry to the church at Corinth centered on a singular question: *Are you sure, Corinthian believers, that you want to stand by the choice you've made?*

This is a key point because, by extension, Paul's question

begs an answer from you and me too. How will we respond to the pains of our age? And decades from now, as we look back on our lives, will we be pleased with the choice that we made?

Perhaps more to the point: Will God himself be pleased?

Across my pastoral years, I've encountered various "models" regarding how believers engage an unbelieving world.[1] Each brings something distinctive to the discussion, but for our purposes here, allow me to pass you my streamlined version of the idea. Based on countless interactions with thousands of Christ followers who yearn to actually follow Christ by living for him in this day and age but who are mystified as to how to get that done, I most often see the following three postures toward relating with a broken world:

1. **The integrators:** those who "go along to get along," who slide effortlessly into the surrounding culture so that they are largely indistinguishable from it.
2. **The instigators:** those who keep a fist raised in anger at those who in their view have abandoned common decency and Judeo-Christian traditions.
3. **The isolators:** those who are so wracked by fear of the troubling trends they see that they go into holy hiding, rarely to be seen or heard from again.

Now, if you're like me, you look at a list like that one and you reflexively think of people you know who fit each category, and then you start judging them for their failures and flaws. We can't help ourselves sometimes, can we? It's terrible to be human sometimes.

But while it is understandably easier to assess other people against these categories, may I suggest we table that task and instead put ourselves through the grid? The question I'd like us to ask ourselves is this one: *If I were to honestly assess my tendencies, which of these three pitfalls do I find most commonly trips me up?*

Do you tend to "go with the flow" of the culture, so that you don't unintentionally rock anyone's boat?

Do you tend to rage against the system, incensed by their depravity and greed?

Do you tend to hunker down and pray that the storm passes?

Which is it for you? For me?

Allow me to round out your understanding of each as you let that question sit in your brain. First, to the integrators.

I read Malcolm Gladwell's book *Outliers: The Story of Success* years ago and remember having a personal epiphany regarding my upbringing in Louisiana. In his chapter "Harlan, Kentucky," Gladwell explores the reasons for the pattern of violence involving families living all along the Appalachian Mountains from the early 1800s until well into the twentieth century and continuing, anecdotally, still today. His contention is that because those living in the southeastern United States are of Scotch-Irish descent, having come to this country from "the lowlands of Scotland, the northern counties of England, and Ulster in Northern Island,"[2] they naturally behave as an "honor culture," a clan that defends the honor of their existence at all costs. Specifically, these folks descended from career herdsmen who were always on the lookout for thieves threatening their cattle or sheep. While the trade may have shifted across the generations, the thinking follows, the fierce protectiveness of one's property, one's livelihood, one's self-worth, remained. Which is why you don't want to offend anyone mired in such a culture; they might just shoot you dead.

As I say, the deeper I got into Gladwell's chapter, the more I understood the town in which I was raised. I grew up in the South. My ancestors all were Welsh, Scottish, or English. And generations ago the vocation they held was herdsmen. Which explains at least in part why, in the county in which I grew up, if you wronged someone, you'd better bet you'd be wronged in return.

By the time I was in the third grade, I'd already been in my fair share of bloody playground battles. My nose had been smashed, my lip had been gashed, and I'd been humiliated more times than seemed fair. And this behavior wasn't relegated to grade-school recess; by that age I'd seen grown women fight. And when I say "fight," I mean *fight*: it was hair-pulling, fist-throwing, donkey-kicking madness. But did I know that it was madness? I did not. This was just the way things were.

My dad was an old-school guy living in the old-school South, where everyone followed a particular set of (admittedly questionable) rules. As I came of age, guess what I then became? *A follower of those same rules.* In response to being bullied in the seventh grade, the advice I received from my adoring father, in short, was "Punch the kid!"

I would go on to do what Dad had advised me to do, but, truly, the only thing I learned by repaying evil with evil was how to be a better violent young man. I developed an edge to my personality that said, *If push comes to shove, I'm in* . . .

I think back on the celebratory dinner that ensued at the Boyd home that night after I'd punched the kid out, and I exhale a sigh of regret. In the South, violence is celebrated as long as that violence is "warranted." Which, by the way, mine was, at least according to everyone on my side. "He had it comin'!" If I heard that phrase once at that family dinner, I heard it a thousand times. "That bully had it comin'!"

As though the rest of us were as pure as the driven snow . . .

I would eventually leave home to head off to college, and then into adulthood, and then into the workforce, and the message that would get reinforced in my heart was, to be crass, "Meekness sucks."

I was from a family that celebrated strength. I was in a circle of friends that celebrated strength. I lived in a nation that celebrated strength. Meekness? Who would ever want *that*?

"Integrators," as I call them, are willing to go along to get along. The thing I was "going along with" in that scenario was the cultural norm that said, "An eye for an eye is good by us!"

Spiritually, integrators are passive. They can be opportunistic, often with few convictions: they have tolerance for sin, and they protect their interests and their people. An example comes to mind of a self-identified Christian mom who, upon learning that her teenage daughter had begun a sexual relationship with the daughter's boyfriend, bought her daughter a bigger bed. "I'd rather encourage them to be here under my roof," she said by way of explanation. "At least I'll know where they are . . ."

Or how about this one: I met a middle-aged man following a service at New Life whom I'd seen sitting next to a woman I presumed was his wife. The man self-identified as a follower of Jesus and then, indicating the woman who'd been with him, said how much they were enjoying worshipping with our church. "Great!" I said. "So, tell me about your wife."

He looked at me sheepishly and said, "Well, she's not my wife . . . she's my girlfriend. But we're living together. It's serious."

"You're living with your girlfriend?" I asked, to which he said, "Yeah, but it's only because if I marry her, she will no longer receive alimony checks from her first husband. With my salary being what it is, we'd never go on another vacation again!"

This is classic integrator behavior. Do you see it? A self-identified believer bends biblically held rules of ethics to yield a desired effect. Whether consciously or subconsciously, integrators integrate into the culture so that they can be accepted by that culture. The integrator will worship with you on Sunday after having cheated on his taxes the week before. The integrator will drink to drunkenness with friends on her back patio, moments after her small

Whether consciously or subconsciously, integrators integrate into the culture so that they can be accepted by that culture.

group leaves. The integrator will tout the benefits of living a moral life even as he engages in serial affairs with women who aren't his wife.

Believers living in Corinth certainly fit this category. In a matter of a handful of years, they had allowed their strong faith in Christ to be diluted by a culture that prized prostitution, drunkenness, and greed. Not knowing how to beat those influences, they simply joined them and never looked back. The apostle Paul had a few things to say about that.

If you picture the will of God as a stream flowing in one direction and the will of the world as a stream flowing in the opposite direction, the analogy I'd make is that the current of modern culture is a raging river, and to try to steady yourself with feet in both waters is to have the world utterly sweep you away.

In my estimation, a full 80 percent of American churchgoers are integrators, Christians in name only, who are being carried along by the culture and who are determined not to make waves. He might stand up for something if he didn't have so much to lose. She has a good job. He has a nice house. She has a solid marriage—or the façade of a solid marriage, anyway. He drives a cool car and has enough discretionary income to go to the Caribbean every year. How could she be expected to give these things up? Yeah, she's not completely comfortable knowing that her boss is cheating on his wife, but live and let live, right? "If I speak up, I could lose my job!" she says in her own defense.

No, the stakes are simply too high for most integrators to change course, and so they sit down, shut their mouths, and coast.

When I was six years old, my grandfather taught me how to trap raccoons. I realize that today this practice is politically incorrect, but, in the deep woods of the South, this is what little boys and their grandpas did. I can still hear Pa's voice ringing in my ears, saying, "Brady, whenever you're in the woods, remember that animals are just like humans: they will always take the path of least resistance. You find the trail, you'll find the 'coons. The last thing they want to do is waste energy fighting through the thicket and brush."

> The stakes are simply too high for most integrators to change course, and so they sit down, shut their mouths, and coast.

That's about the best word picture of the integrators I can think of. They want the most return for the least amount of effort, even as that path of least resistance leads them closer and closer toward death.

Let's continue on with the isolators.

If you caught M. Night Shyamalan's 2004 film, *The Village*, then you've seen isolationism in action. In the movie a small band of residents live secluded in a remote Pennsylvania town, ostensibly in the eighteenth or nineteenth century, and are forbidden from venturing into the surrounding woods. But when people fall ill and medical supplies are needed, the Elders of the town at last allow one resident, a blind girl, to make the "dangerous" trek through the woods to seek help.

What we learn as that young woman reaches the perimeter of the village is that it is actually the Walker Wildlife Preserve, founded in the 1970s by one of the Elders, Edward Walker, who was a professor at the University of Pennsylvania, and the residents are living in current times. Walker had been so leveled by the murder of his father that he approached others in his grief-recovery class to see if they would join him in creating a protected environment, where the world could hurt them no more.

Walker used his family fortune to purchase the land, pay off the government to declare the area a no-fly zone, and cover the salaries of multiple "park rangers," who ensured that no outside forces penetrated the perimeter. From there, he and the other Elders went to great lengths—even creating the illusion of "monsters" that inhabited the forest—to keep up the façade, which sounds rather unbelievable unless you understand how the mind of an isolator works.

In the nonfiction world, I have seen isolator parents create a bubbled environment for their kids by refusing to let them play with friends, engage in extracurricular activities, or see movies in a movie theater. I have seen isolator parents protect their children from reading any library book that could be considered "worldly." I have seen isolator families relocate from suburbia to a multi-acre homestead and unplug from the world on their way there. Isolators eye the culture through the lens of fear. *They've lost their way,* isolators think, *and there is no hope for them now.*

You may encounter them in the "real world," but you'll rarely see them engage. They are the ones listening politely as you ramble on about the latest TV show you're binge-watching or the delicious wine you just discovered, while inside they have no idea what you are talking about.

If you were to talk with a group of isolators about Jesus' injunction to "go into all the world and make disciples of all nations," the Great Commission we looked at earlier, you might detect trepidation on their part. Things in the world have spiraled out of control in their view. They feel safer holing away than engaging with folks "out there," which presents a real problem for them, since "out there" is the world they are called to serve and love and reach with the Good News of Christ. Isolators' private, protected worlds take precedent over *the* world to which Jesus referred.

Isolators' private, protected worlds take precedent over *the* world to which Jesus referred.

Last year an isolator took me to task after a Sunday service because I made a passing reference in my sermon to Pikes Peak being "millions of years old." To say that this person was outraged is no exaggeration; you'd have thought I insulted his kid's intelligence, considering the icy reception I received. "Pastor Brady," he said, "how could you *betray* us? I thought you were a young-earther all this time!"

Listen, whether the earth is five thousand years old or millions of years old or somewhere in between, to put so much weight on a negotiable aspect of theology is a fool's errand and nothing more. Unless we come together, we will die apart. After spending several minutes in conversation with the man, I asked if we could agree to disagree and still move forward in unity. Thankfully, he said yes.

My plea to isolators is to think carefully about how long

it has been since they were around someone who thinks totally differently from them. When was the last time they had someone over for dinner who didn't adhere to their political beliefs? When was the last time they engaged someone in conversation who was apathetic—or even antagonistic—toward the claims of Christ? Jesus was serious when he entrusted the spread of the gospel to individual lives, individual hearts. He expected that we would choose to come together so that his bride, the church, would thrive. To shrug our shoulders at his request and move ahead with our segregation plan is a terrible choice to make. Yes, we can hole away with people who look just like we look, vote just like we vote, spend just like we spend, and worship just like we do and name it something like "protecting our heritage," but the cold, hard fact remains: this is isolationism at its finest. And there's nothing fine about that.

Jesus was serious when he entrusted the spread of the gospel to individual lives, individual hearts. He expected that we would choose to come together so that his bride, the church, would thrive.

There is a third tack I often see believers living in an unbelieving world take, which is to become instigators, those who stir up trouble as if for sport. These are the moral crusaders among us who are so entranced with cursing the darkness that lighting a candle seems an absurd thing to do.

I have a real soft spot for instigators, being a recovering instigator myself. Instigators, generally pharisaical in their approach, believe that as a society we are losing something that is sacred to us and that it is our generation's responsibility to recover that particular thing. "Not on *our* watch!" they shout. "We must *not* let the culture win!"

Win what? I always want to ask. *What, exactly, has been lost?*

I know people who are forever pining for America "as it used to be." On my bolder days, I counter their reminiscing with something along the lines of *You do realize that the nostalgia you long for involved black people being made to drink from different water fountains than white people, right?*

This country hasn't exactly been the model of upright behavior regarding how it treats anyone who doesn't look like a well-resourced middle-aged white guy.

"Do you realize that health care is much better now?" I sometimes add, in these conversations with those longing for the good old days. "And that women have more rights? And that we elected our first black president . . ."

These are the moral crusaders among us who are so entranced with cursing the darkness that lighting a candle seems an absurd thing to do.

I'll tell you at the outset that whenever I lay out this last category for believers, I am met with a fair amount of resistance. "I wouldn't be this angry if people weren't so crazy!"

The "crazy people" run the gamut: they might be gay people, homeschooling people, liberal people, pro-Palestinian people, pro-choice people, Republican people, megachurch people (guess how I know) . . . I've found with instigators that it matters less *who* is the enemy than that there *is* a shared enemy to unite against. And while it's true that instigators will prize evangelism in theory, in practice they care little about the souls they say they're trying to save. "Plus, what's so bad about devoting yourself to influencing this world for good?" Instigators continue, puffs of smoke still emerging from their ears. I understand their point, but the truth is this: when you are motivated by anger and rage, you eventually resort to employing the same tactics—shame, embarrassment, vitriol, humiliation, guilt—in your effort to bring about change that the other side is using to keep that change from occurring.

The kingdom of God isn't ushered in by vitriol or guilt. It is ushered in solely by love.

More succinctly, the kingdom of God isn't ushered in by vitriol or guilt. It is ushered in solely by love.

In case you're still undecided about which category most accurately depicts your reaction to a world that isn't all that enamored with the person, power, or claims of Jesus, let me give a thought experiment to consider. Suppose for a moment that your brother texts to say he'll be in town for the wedding of a friend who happens to live in your same zip code and wonders if he can crash at your house. You love your brother. You rarely get to see your brother. You immediately respond with "Anytime! Come on . . ."

Your brother arrives into town and, after catching up for a bit, says, "Hey, you're welcome to come to this wedding with me tonight." He laughs and adds, "I forgot to pack a date."

You have nothing planned, so you agree to go. Once seated at the ceremony, you notice a preponderance of gay couples in the crowd. This makes sense to you once you catch sight of the wedding couple: two men.

Now, depending on which category you most often find yourself in, you will have a clear reaction to this turn of events. Would you storm out? Would you feel nauseated and angry? Would you barely notice or barely care that you'd attended a gay wedding? Would you avoid contact with your brother, who was obviously complicit in this whole thing, for years to come? Which reaction aligns with how *you'd* feel?

"I tell you how *I'd* feel!" the instigator hollers. "I'd be outraged—that's how I'd feel."

"To each his own," the integrator says. "Am I right?"

"That was the day my brother and I stopped staying in touch," says the isolator. "Yes, I'll always love him, but clearly we're just living *very* different lives . . ."

Awareness of the culture allows me to engage in a loving manner with those *in* the culture; anger toward it puts a wall up between them and me.

Listen, while this scenario is hypothetical, situations like this one unfold every day of our lives, in thousands upon thousands of ways. And the results of people's reactions to those situations can be quite dramatic, consequential, potentially devastating, and sad. Because once we paint ourselves into a corner—whether driven there by fear, by conforming, or by rage—it is extraordinarily difficult to get out.

It seems fitting to mention here that my wife and I have two teenagers, a son and a daughter, and that I am *very* concerned about the world they are inheriting as they come into adulthood. It's just that I'm not angry about it. And the difference between the two is significant. Awareness *of* the culture allows me to engage in a loving manner with those *in* the culture; anger toward it puts a wall up between them and me.

I see myriad similarities between the apostle Paul's circumstances and the world you and I are living in today, not the least among them the fact that we value independence, upward mobility, the shiny, the slick, and the new. We prefer to define morality on our own terms, truth on our own terms, success on our own terms, and wisdom on our own terms, and yet there stands Jesus with a far different view on things. *There is a kind of wisdom,* we remember Paul saying, *that trumps the worldly wisdom you prize. But it is only accessible through the person of Christ. It is found only by looking to him.*

And so, this book: in these pages I have done my level best to lay out the wisdom that trumps our perspective on things. Let me assure you, as you dive into the following chapters, that regardless of which category you find yourself in, you can get better at thinking and looking and acting like the person of Christ.

Instigators can learn to express their vision for their family, their neighborhood, their city, their country, and the world without expressing anger toward any one individual or demonizing any particular group.

Integrators can learn to demonstrate remarkably noble behavior that sets them apart from the crowd in which they run.

Isolators can learn to initiate, invest in, and even relish relationships with people who differ from them spiritually, politically, emotionally, educationally, financially, and more.

These strides aren't just possible, I must tell you; they are *probable* for those committed to living the way of Christ.

When I was a young man of twenty-two years, my favorite book of the Bible was the book of James. I would sit at my desk and read those five chapters, finish, and read them again. I was incredibly drawn to the concepts I found there, even as they wrecked me every time.

In James 1:22 (NIV), one of the many verses that I memorized during that season of growth, we read these words: "Do not merely listen to the word, and so deceive yourselves. Do what it says." Every time I read those two sentences, I'd stop and exhale, just captivated by the thought of steering clear of self-deception simply by doing what the Bible said to do.

It sounds so simple, right? Truthfully, I think it is. Our problem is that we get tangled up in debates about whether Adam had a belly button or where the dinosaurs all went or exactly how old planet Earth may be, and we lose the plot of what life is supposed to be about. Sure, it can be a lot of fun to debate the mysteries of Scripture, but not at the expense of acting on that which is clear. To be knowers of God's Word but not doers is the equivalent of inhaling all day but never exhaling. Which would be a ridiculous way to try to stay alive.

This book is a *breathing* book, an opportunity to inhale and exhale alike. It is an invitation to encounter the Scriptures afresh; to explore the topics that threatened to rip apart the church at Corinth, which happen to be the very same ones beating down our doors today; to embrace a *fourth* approach that we can have to a culture that has no use for God, an approach centered on the wisdom not of this world but of God; and to emerge remarkable followers of Christ. We can learn to be not merely hearers of the Word but also doers. Really. The whole lot of us can. We can reclaim the peace, the freedom, the joy that pigeonholing ourselves in our buckets of instigation, integration, and isolation have stolen. And, leaning into the vision the apostle Paul held for lovers of God, we can let love guide our every step.

3

The Fourth Way

We Can Be a People of Remarkable Love

The best use of life is love.

RICK WARREN

A fascinating story appears in Mark 5 that centers on Jesus, his disciples, and a deeply troubled man. To set the stage, the text says that Jesus had been ministering to the masses on one side of a lake and then told his disciples that he wanted to go "to the other side" (Mark 4:35). During the men's crossing, a fierce storm erupted, its high waves crashed onto the boat, and the boat began to take on water. Through it all, Jesus was evidently sleeping in the back of the boat, but soon enough his terrified disciples shook him awake saying, "Teacher, don't you care that we're going to drown?" (v. 38), to which Jesus responded first not to the men but to the waves. "Silence!" he said. "Be still!" (v. 39). After what Mark describes as a "great calm" unfolded across the lake, Jesus looked at his followers and said, "Why are you afraid? Do you still have no faith?" (v. 40).

Who was this man, Jesus' disciples wondered, who could command both water and wind?

The men eventually made it to the other side to a region called Gerasenes, even as the welcome that awaited them was less than warm:

> *When Jesus climbed out of the boat, a man possessed by an evil spirit came out from the tombs to meet him. This man lived in the burial caves and could no longer be restrained, even with a chain. Whenever he was put into chains and shackles—as he often was—he snapped the chains from his wrists and smashed the shackles. No one was strong enough to subdue him. Day and night he wandered among the burial caves and in the hills, howling and cutting himself sharp stones [vv. 2–5].*

The picture here is one of distaste—revulsion, even. How would Jesus choose to respond?

Reading further, we learn that the troubled man longs for help. "When Jesus was still some distance away," the text says, "the man saw him, ran to meet him, and bowed low before him. With a shriek, he screamed, 'Why are you interfering with me, Jesus, Son of the Most High God? In the name of God, I beg you, don't torture me!' For Jesus had already said to the spirit, 'Come out of the man, you evil spirit.'

"Then Jesus demanded, 'What is your name?'" (vv. 6–9).

Again, the man speaks: "'My name is Legion, because there are many of us inside this man.' Then the evil spirits begged him again and again not to send them to some distant place" (vv. 9–10).

As if the story isn't strange enough already, Jesus then honors the demons' request to be sent into a nearby herd of pigs that are feeding on a hillside nearby. It is better than any other alternative, they figure, and to their immense relief Jesus complies. The result? Some two thousand pigs plunge into the water and drown in the lake below. So there's that.

But there's also this, according to Mark 5:15: "A crowd soon gathered around Jesus, and they saw the man who had been possessed by the legion of demons. He was sitting there fully clothed and perfectly sane, and they were all afraid."

After what they'd seen? Yeah, fear was a reasonable response. Calming a storm was one thing; moving not away from but *toward* someone they deemed unworthy of inclusion and fellowship? This was a different thing altogether.

Their question stood: *Who was this man?*

More on that in a moment.

When the apostle Paul arrived in Corinth, the Corinthians had already heard about him. To be a Christ follower in Asia or Greece in that day was to be familiar with all the apostles, who were considered spiritual directors, enlightened sojourners, faithful guides. Such guidance was coveted, because although these people had discovered the story of Jesus and had committed themselves to following Jesus, it is likely that these members of a new church—a tiny house church—hadn't yet been discipled. They hadn't had anyone explain to them the implications of that story or the ways in which that followership should occur. There were no formal denominational structures to lean into, no church buildings to visit, no "professional pastors" to seek out. If these believers were going to experience spiritual formation—if they were going to learn the bedrock foundations of the faith—it was going to happen by way of someone such as Paul. Which is perhaps why this church in Corinth had sent Paul a letter containing the various issues that perplexed them. In response, Paul showed up.

At the core of the Corinthians' primary concerns was how to live soberly in a drunken world. The Corinthian culture was drunk on power, drunk on success, drunk on indulgence, drunk on self. They had little use for God, it seemed, or for anything that he stood for. How was the church supposed to respond to these trends? What were believers to do?

Take, for example, the issue of food sacrificed to idols. We know that the church included in their letter to Paul their concern regarding whether to eat such food because of Paul's direct response: "Now regarding your question about food that has been offered to idols," he wrote in 1 Corinthians 8:1. "Yes, we know that 'we all have knowledge' about this issue."

What was happening here was that heathen priests were taking meat into pagan temples and offering it to false gods before turning around and selling that meat in town. You'll recall that at the same time these sacrifices were occurring, spreading throughout the immediate temple area, men were employing the services of a reported thousand "sacred prostitutes" before returning home to their wife and kids.[1] Believers easily discerned that sexual compromise was immoral, but was it okay to eat compromised meat?

I imagine that some said, "We can't even *touch* that meat. It's been offered up to false gods!" While others said, "Who cares if it's been offered to false gods? Those gods don't even *exist*." They surely wondered how Paul would respond.

Let me push pause on this scene for a moment and bring the issue closer to home. You'll recall that the church at Corinth was made up both of Gentiles and Jews, and if I had to guess, I'd say the line of demarcation for that eat/don't eat discussion fell between those two camps. For Jews, who were accustomed to vast and detailed laws concerning the meaning, preparation, and consumption of food, knowing that the cow had been slain before Aphrodite's statue prior to the steak making its way to their plates would have been highly problematic for them. Good Jews didn't worship false gods, and they didn't eat animals that had been in those gods' presence.

Now, my assumption is that "food that has been offered to idols" isn't a real hot-button issue for you today. You might like your beef grass-finished, your chicken free-range, and your pork humanely raised, but my guess is that you have never once concerned yourself with whether those animals were used in pagan rituals prior to showing up at your local grocery store.

But that doesn't mean you don't have a hot button to push. What do *you* find revolting these days? What would the opening statement of Paul's letter of response have sounded like for *you*?

"Now, regarding your question about women in leadership . . ."

"Now, regarding your question about that 'homeschool threat' . . ."

"Now, regarding your question about gay marriage . . ."

"Now, regarding your question about Tea Partiers . . ."

"Now, regarding your question about those who have transitioned . . ."

"Now, regarding your question about conservative talk-radio hosts . . ."

"Now, regarding your question about those who use recreational marijuana . . ."

"Now, regarding your question about those coming to your country illegally . . ."

"Now, regarding your question about those who voted for Donald Trump . . ."

Do we engage with such people or not?

The way to reclaim sanity in any situation is to take a step forward in love.

It should be no surprise that Paul's counsel to the church mirrored Jesus' approach to that troubled man on the other side of the lake. "While knowledge makes us feel important," Paul wrote, "it is love that strengthens the church" (1 Corinthians 8:1).

As in: "Yes, we all know that these people are sacrificing food to idols. Yes, we all know that you find this immoral, distasteful, wrong. Yes, we all know that this is a hot button for you. Yes, *still* I'm asking you to love."

The way to reclaim sanity in any situation is to take a step forward in love.

In response to what the Corinthian believers thought was a black-or-white question, Paul's insight must have seemed gray.

"Do we eat the food or not, Paul?"

"Church at Corinth, always choose love."

Huh?

The tendencies those believers felt are the same ones we wrestle with still today. Whenever we encounter something we find distasteful in the world around us, we, too, are tempted to denigrate, downplay, or run. Instigators will rise in righteous anger and *denigrate* the powers that be. Integrators will *downplay* the depth of the dysfunction, even joining in with the madness over time. And isolators will simply run for their lives, holing away until brighter days dawn. "There is a fourth way," Paul was reminding them, "and that way is marked by love."

For the instigators in this situation, the Jews, the implications here involved refraining from judging those in their midst. "Knowledge puffs up while love builds up," Paul reminded them in 1 Corinthians 8:1 (NIV), but "[t]hose who think they know something do not yet know as they ought to know" (v. 2). In another of his letters, this one to the church at Philippi, Paul instructed believers to, yes, acknowledge conduct that stands as an enemy of Christ so long as they did so *with tears in their eyes* (see Philippians 3:18).

For the integrators, the Gentiles, the implications of Paul's counsel involved being careful not to lead another believer astray. "For if others see you—with your 'superior knowledge'—eating in the temple of an idol," Paul reasoned, "won't they be encouraged to violate their conscience by eating food that has been offered to an idol? . . . And when you sin against other believers by encouraging them to do something they believe is wrong, you are sinning against Christ. So if what I eat causes another believer to sin, I will never eat meat again as long as I live—for I don't want to cause another believer to stumble" (1 Corinthians 8:10, 12–13).

For any isolators who may have been in hiding when the letter was sent to Paul, he said, "the person who loves God is the one whom God recognizes" (v. 3). But it's kind of hard to love God when you refuse to engage with the people he made . . .

Love, love, love, was the drum Paul seemed to beat. Whenever you're wondering how to reflect Jesus to a hurting world, the answer is always love.

Chances are, you've been to a Christian wedding, and chances are, at that Christian wedding, you heard a familiar passage of Scripture read. At least in modern times, it seems the quintessential go-to text for the occasion of a bride and groom becoming one is 1 Corinthians 13, otherwise known as "Paul's Hymn to Love." And for good reason: Who in a right mind *wouldn't* want a spouse who never gets irritable, who never gets jealous, and who never keeps track of your wrongs?

In fact, these well-known verses—"Love is patient, love is kind" and so forth (NIV)—were not written to husbands and wives. Not to burst any bubbles, but the "love chapter" that is so often read at Christian weddings has nothing to do with marriage. The context here is the *church*; Paul's instruction was for the church. With that in mind, let's revisit what Paul had to say.

"If I speak in the tongues of men or of angels," Paul wrote, "but do not have love, I am only a resounding gong or a clanging cymbal. If I have the gift of prophecy and can fathom all mysteries and all knowledge, and if I have a faith that can move mountains, but do not have love, I am nothing. If I give all I possess to the poor and give my body over to hardship that I may boast, but do not have love, I gain nothing" (1 Corinthians 13:1–3, NIV).

Let me stop us for a brief consideration: Imagine for a moment that you could do these things that Paul is talking about. You could *speak in the tongues of men and angels*. You could *fathom all mysteries and all knowledge*. You could *have faith that can move mountains*. You could *give all you possess to the poor*. You could *give your body over to hardship*, courageously being burned at the stake as a martyr. I don't know about you, but I find this to be a pretty impressive list. If I ever met someone who could do even three of these five, I'd for sure want to hang out with them. If I knew someone who consistently did even *one* of these things, I'd think, *Now,* that *is an admirable trait.*

And yet, God is not impressed.

You can do all these spiritually impressive things, and yet, *without love, you've got nothing at all.* In the words of the late Eugene H. Peterson, we're "bankrupt without love" (1 Corinthians 13:7, MSG). The language of this new kingdom that Jesus was ushering in, this new citizenship of heaven, is *love*: not the self-focused love the Greeks were accustomed to—love as licentiousness or weapon or tool—but a *love that seeks to serve.*

The implications of this shift were severe. To help those believers—and also us—know whether they'd made the shift, Paul offered up a handful of ways to tell. In the same way that figs hanging from a tree reveal the type of tree that it is, six clear-cut characteristics reveal that that person belongs to Christ.

Love is patient and kind.

Paul's first description of love was this: "Love is patient and kind"—or, in the Amplified Bible, "Love endures with patience and serenity, love is kind and thoughtful . . ." (1 Corinthians 13:4, AMP). And while, at face value, these concepts seem reasonable to us, you have to remember that the people to whom Paul was speaking lived in the shadow of a violent Roman regime. Values such as patience and kindness weren't exactly the norm. Jesus' teachings in his Sermon on the Mount, which serve as the basis for Paul's comments here, were seen as radical departures because they *indeed radically departed* from the ways of life back then.

In the Jewish culture, scholars believe, most everyone was right-hand dominant. People ate with their right hands. They gripped with their right hands. They struck with their right hands. You may recall that one of Jesus' exhortations was that, despite people having heard that "the law . . . says the punishment must match the injury: 'An eye for an eye, and a tooth for a tooth,'" they should instead choose not to resist the evil person behind the affront (Matthew 5:38). "If someone slaps you on the right cheek," Jesus said, "offer the other cheek also" (v. 39).

Now, think about what he's saying. If I'm right-handed, and you're right-handed, and you slap me "on the right cheek," the only way you're going to get that done is by backhanding me across the face. If you backhanded me across the face, I'll admit that I'd be upset. But if I were a Jew living in Jesus' day? I'd be appalled. Outraged. *Incensed.* To backhand someone in the first century was to convey that they were less than human, that they were worthy of being treated like a dog. The human-nature reaction to being backhanded is to flatten your hand and slap back. And yet this is the opposite of what Jesus advised.

"That's not the kingdom I came to usher in," Jesus pointed out. "My kingdom is built on *peace*."

Despite how shocking this news must have seemed, Jesus was far from done.

"If you are sued in court," he continued, "and your shirt is taken from you, give your coat, too" (v. 40). One layer you could give and still be clothed, right? But both layers? Now you're cold.

Still Jesus was not done.

"If a soldier demands that you carry his gear for a mile, carry it two miles" (v. 41). The Romans were the first civilization to put mile markers on the highways that they themselves had built. Jesus' audience knew *precisely* what this instruction meant.

By law, if a soldier of the Roman army was walking along the highway and spotted you standing there, he could require you to take all his armor and equipment for the length of one mile. There was no way out of providing this "assistance." This was the law; it was how things worked. Jesus' counsel? Don't fight it. In fact, go *two* miles instead of one.

These ideas weren't floated as suggestions, as you can see. They were presented as *the way things ought to be*. This was to be the new normal, by the Spirit's empowerment: the new system, the new deal. Evidently, the One who could calm the wind and the waves could make peaceful the human heart too.

Love is not jealous or boastful or proud or rude.

Paul's next phrase (verse 42) was this: "Love is not jealous or boastful or proud or rude," and while those words certainly were relevant for the ego-stroked culture of Corinth, with its new-money wealth and newfound prominence, its shamelessness, grandiosity, and pride, the sentiment goes for the jugular with us too. We could stand some improvement here.

You've probably noticed that we live in a follow-me world. Follow me on Instagram. Follow me on Facebook. Follow me on Twitter. Follow me wherever I go. We think this is a new phenomenon, or at least only as old as is social media. Paul confirms that it's a long-standing issue: rampant self-interest and pride. "If you're going to be part of this new kingdom that Jesus is ushering into planet Earth," he said, "then you will need to learn this new posture, one of others-centeredness and not centeredness on self."

A friend of mine calls this near-universal tendency we feel to elevate oneself the "Me monster."

In Paul's view, it's a monster that ought to be slain.

In the gospel of Mark, we read these words from Jesus: "When you pray, don't be like the hypocrites who love to pray publicly on the street corners and in the synagogues where everyone can see them. I tell you the truth, that is all the reward they will ever get. But when you pray, go away by yourself, shut the door behind you, and pray to your Father in private. Then your Father, who sees everything, will reward you.

"When you pray, don't babble on and on as the Gentiles do. They think their prayers are answered merely by repeating their words again and again. Don't be like them, for your Father knows exactly what you need even before you ask him!" (Mark 6:5–8).

In Proverbs 27:1–2, Solomon, an Old Testament king who once was considered the wisest man ever to live, wrote, "Don't brag about tomorrow, since you don't know what the day will bring. Let someone else praise you, not your own mouth—a stranger, not your own lips."

I've said to more than a few friends, only partially in jest, "Man, I'd sure love to brag about you, but you keep beating me to the punch . . ."

Too often, I'm guilty of the same.

A verse I committed to memory years ago, I rely on still today: "So humble yourselves under the mighty power of God," 1 Peter 5:6 says, "and at the right time he will lift you up in honor."

We need not brag on ourselves; *the Lord will lift us up.*

These days, whenever I walk into a place of business or into a restaurant or into someone else's home, I remind myself, *Brady, don't be boastful. The Lord will lift you up. Work to draw out the other person's story and experience. The Lord will honor you.*

That simple reminder is incredibly helpful to me. On social media, I try to follow the same rule by asking myself, *Why am I posting this or responding to this? What's my motive here? Am I trying to elevate myself so that people will like or respect me? Or am I trying to glorify God?*

If you'd like a starting point along these lines, I encourage you work over the next seven days to turn every conversation away from yourself. Just for one week, stop making everything about you. Ask about people's stories. Ask about their work. Ask about their families. Ask about their dreams. Respond to their questions in accordance with a natural give-and-take, but then turn the spotlight back toward them. And then, at week's end, take stock. How do you feel? What did you learn? Why might love necessitate an intentional focus away from ourselves?

Love does not demand its own way.

While there are many drawbacks to getting older, one of the decided benefits is that peacefulness has its way. If you're open to the work of Christ's transformation in your life, then one of the things that happens as you age is that you feel a deeper sense of gratitude for the grace you've received along the way. You see the mistakes you've made with greater clarity. You see your fallenness in sharper relief. You accept your limitations with greater compassion. You feel more appreciative, more serene. And with this newfound sense of steadiness, you can't help but pass it on. I guess what I'm saying is that I'm less prone to outrage as a fifty-two-year-old than I was in my younger years. I'm less "demanding"—what a great way to put it! To Paul's point here, I don't fight for "my way."

In the last chapter, I posed a hypothetical scenario that's less and less hypothetical all the time. Your brother comes to visit and invites you to come along to a wedding he's attending that night with two grooms. If you're an isolator or an instigator, then you're most assuredly going to demand "your way." You'll either write off your brother from that day forward, or else cause a scene as you storm out of the room. If you're an integrator, then you'll simply join in on the fun, barely registering that anything's amiss. But can I draw our attention to this "fourth way" of love? Can we play with an outcome here?

At that wedding reception, instead of papering the wall with your presence, hiding the fact that you're a believer, or stoking the sense of outrage you feel deep inside, you join your brother as he approaches the happy couple to congratulate them. You stick out your hand, introduce yourself, and say, "Hey, thanks for letting me crash your party. I hear we're neighbors . . . Good to meet you guys."

You're not compromising your core convictions, but neither are you condemning anyone or anything. You're simply *engaging,* in love, in Christ's likeness . . . You're simply choosing to show up and stay.

A few moments later you learn that your brother's friends hang out at the same coffee shop you frequent, and so you mention that you hope to bump into them sometime. They're energized by the idea and tell you to get their contact information from your brother. And then *you actually do*. You follow up a few weeks later. You invite them to coffee—your treat. You start to learn about their lives and their work, and a friendship begins to emerge.

They're not a project.

They're not a mission field.

They're not a conversion that's reliant on you.

They're simply two guys whose path has crossed your path in life, and you're being faithful to love them well.

For two thousand–plus years, Christ's followers have been at their best when working the margins of society as a minority, not when operating as a powerhouse. Anytime Christians have been handed power, they have squandered it like all people do. No, far better to assume a place of humility there on the fringes, where we need the Spirit in order to thrive. You want to see the kingdom of heaven breaking through on the earth? Open arms. Open heart. Genuine smile.

For two thousand–plus years, Christ followers have been at their best when working the margins of society as a minority.

Love "doesn't force itself on others" and doesn't have to be "me-first," the *Message* version of this idea reads (1 Corinthians 13:5, MSG). *Love loves to celebrate others,* I take that verse to mean, *no matter who they are.* Lay down your preferences and choose to engage. Accept all people, right where they are. Counter the way of egotism . . . For once, don't demand your own way.

Love is not irritable and keeps no record of being wronged.

The trend starts when we're little kids, doesn't it?

> *Mom:* "Johnny, why did you eat your brother's donut?"
> *Johnny:* "Because he ate mine last time!"

Certainly, as violations become more consequential than a donut snatched from our grasp, we must take pains to get that issue resolved. But for everyday slights, we do better to choose to start fresh every time we cross paths. "There's a difference between good judgment and living in judgment," author Bob Goff says. "The trick is to use lots of the first and to go a little lighter on the second . . ."[2]

Resolve issues as they crop up, with forgiveness and grace, and let the past remain in the past.

Love does not rejoice about injustice but rejoices whenever the truth wins out.

Before I fully surrendered my life to Christ, I entertained some truly horrific habits. At the same time that I was indulging my every last sinful desire, I happened to have some friends who were living far more righteous lives. I couldn't help but notice that those friends did not judge me, a young man who was not yet following Christ, for doing things that weren't Christlike. Isn't that uncanny? They didn't expect me to act like Jesus, because I was not yet following Jesus.

I learned something from those guys. When we encounter people who do not profess to know, love, or follow Jesus Christ, the last thing we should do is expect them to look and act like Jesus Christ. This progression might have slipped from your recollection, but everyone who has ever become a Christian has been cleansed of her or his sin only after first coming to Jesus Christ. We come and *then* we're cleansed. We can't get clean before we come.

This fifth fruit of love, according to the apostle Paul has two parts to it. Love "does not rejoice at injustice," 1 Corinthians 13:6 (AMP) says, "but rejoices with the truth [when right and truth prevail]." Part one of Paul's description reminds us never to snicker at wickedness and sin. Those friends I had when I was in my late teens and into my twenties were careful to honor those words. They certainly didn't approve of how I was living my life, even as they refused to judge me for the choices I made. This was a loving posture for them to take, as it turns out. I felt equal parts accepted and prompted toward my potential in Christ. What a gift that balance was!

But there's a second part here, which is just as important as the first: Love also "rejoices with the truth," Paul says, meaning that it takes pleasure as spiritual progress gets made.

In our day, we have so merged our spiritual beliefs with our political beliefs that we can no longer tell the difference between the two. Case in point: when we can no longer see the good in someone because we disagree with his or her political stance, we know we've crossed a point of no return. We'd better throw it in reverse—and fast.

It is true that sometimes we need to acknowledge redemptive potential from a distance, such as when dealing with an abuser, a pathological liar, or "tricky people," as they're sometimes called. "When someone shows you who they are, believe them the first time,"[3] Maya Angelou once wisely said. And indeed, that's what we should do. But in *all* cases we must see the humanity in humans. We must honor the "God" in them. Love demands that we hold out hope for them so that *spiritual progress can still get made.*

Everyone who has ever become a Christian has been cleansed of her or his sin only after first coming to Jesus Christ.

Which brings us to point number six.

Love never gives up, never loses faith, is always hopeful, and endures through every circumstance.

Finally, the apostle Paul says that "love never gives up, never loses faith, is always hopeful, and endures through every circumstance" (1 Corinthians 13:7). In other words, *love always perseveres.* If point five was about a certain posture to assume toward those living far from God, then point six is about how long to hold that posture—in a word, *forever*. Essentially, Paul was saying, "I have made the decision to show love in every situation, regardless of what ensues from there. On good days and bad, in situations both affirming and costly, on every occasion and with everyone, I for one choose love. I will love others today. I will love others tomorrow. I will love others ten years from now. For as long as these lungs are taking in air, love is the oxygen I choose to breathe."

He hopes we'll make the same wise choice.

Let me tell you why this issue of perseverance is important. Say you come to my home for dinner one night and meet my family for the first time. Unbeknownst to you, my wife, Pam, has had a root canal that day, Abram is swamped with homework, Callie is grieving her best friend having recently moved away, and I had two highly valuable senior staff members up and quit that afternoon. Now, you don't know that any of these things have occurred. You think it has been an average day for the Boyd household and are looking forward to meeting my wife and kids.

Pam and the kids and I put on a brave face for an hour or so, but eventually our façades slide down. Pam can barely talk because her mouth is throbbing in pain. Abram doesn't really engage because his mind keeps drifting to the paper he needs to write. Callie is distant and seems apathetic. I'm dreading a call to the elders I need to make. We're tired. We're grieving. We're overwhelmed and in various states of distress. Mostly, we just want to go to bed. But we're trying to be gracious—really, we are. We like you. We just don't want you here now.

Let me ask you a question: As you drive home that evening, what will your impression be of my family? Will you have found us to be welcoming and loving like Jesus? Or will you come away thinking we're a little sullen, a little angry, a little weird?

The reason that perseverance is necessary is because transformation happens over time. In the same way that drawing conclusions about my family based on one three-hour segment of time won't necessarily yield an accurate assessment of the Holy Spirit's activity in our lives, choosing to judge others based on chance encounters, social media posts, and what's reported in the news can't adequately sum up their relationship with God. If you've ever watched a chrysalis turn into a butterfly, then you know that you can stare at that thing every day and see nothing worth cheering about. But then, eventually, the pod starts to open, releasing beauty and grandeur and flight. To assess a person in a moment is to be disheartened by humanity yet again. But to stick with that person over a *season*, over an *era*, over *real time*, is to see real progress made.

I have seen my wife on a bad day. I have seen my son and my daughter on a bad day. They have seen me on more bad days than I've cared to have. But guess what we know about each other? We know that each of us is a beautiful vessel of Holy Spirit–empowered activity, and that despite our foibles and failings we are growing leaps and bounds in Christ. How do I know this? Because we've *persevered*. We've given each other the gift of time.

On this theme of waiting for each other, of persisting until growth has its way, theologian Joseph Parker writes, "It is weakness that stops the house, it is the baby that keeps the family at home; it is the lame limb that detains all the sound faculties and says, 'Stop! What! Am I to stop because I have one lame limb? I am sound in all my other limbs, and sound in all my mental faculties, and am I to be humbled in this way?'

"Yes, you are, and you cannot get out of it. So the Apostle [Paul] says, 'Here is a lame man in the Church, and the Church must wait for him'; and the Church says, 'This is the singular pass we have come to, all waiting for one lame man.' The Apostle says, 'That is the very idea of the Church. The whole universe may be waiting for one little lame world called the earth: nobody can tell how fast the universe might get on but for this cripple called the earth.' "[4]

True, the Bible may not say all the things we wish it would say, but it does indeed say things we need. And at the top of that list, I have to believe, is this prompting toward Christlike love. Despite our differences, despite our convictions, despite our preferences and perspectives and pain—at the end of it all, we are told to love God, and to love *all* with neighborly love.

From the beginning pages of Scripture right until today, God has wanted to have a people of his own possession who were holy and set apart, a people who would follow hard after him, desiring only the things he desired. It's an option that's still available to us, if only we'll decide not to be merely engaged with Jesus but instead by him to be *consumed*.

He never sinned,
nor ever deceived anyone.
He did not retaliate when he was insulted,
nor threaten revenge when he suffered.
He left his case in the hands of God,
who always judges fairly.
He personally carried our sins
in his body on the cross
so that we can be dead to sin
and live for what is right.
By his wounds
you are healed.
Once you were like sheep
who wandered away.
But now you have turned to your Shepherd,
the Guardian of your souls.

—1 Peter 2:22–25

This. This is love.

4

Distinctly One

We Can Exhibit Remarkable Equality

All animals are equal, but some animals
are more equal than others.

GEORGE ORWELL

Two years ago, for the first time in my eleven-year tenure at New Life, we as a church experienced something of a financial breakthrough. We'd been through the scandalous departure of our founding pastor and, one hundred days into my filling the role of senior pastor, a shooting that took the lives of two of our teenagers. The fallout from those two tragedies had been severe, flattening both our attendance and our giving trends. Making matters worse was the $26 million in debt I inherited upon coming to the church. I was committed to paying that total down even as I knew it would be a tough sell.

Asking people to give money to "debt reduction" is every bit as enjoyable as it seems, but I kept assuring our congregation that once we had a little breathing room we would give to far more exciting things. As it turned out, most trusted that what I was saying was true. They gave, and our debt load decreased. In due time, our finance chief and I were shaking our heads in humble disbelief that not only had that total been whittled to $12 million but, for the first time in a long time, the church had significant cash on hand.

As an executive team, we believed that it was time to expand our reach. Not only did we possess the leadership capital necessary, but we had the financial capital now too. We were committed to increasing our ability to serve the city in which we live; the only question that remained was *how*. We had launched extensions downtown and west of town that were both thriving; the consideration now was where to go next. North and east of us, communities were popping up seemingly overnight, which meant that if we positioned a campus in one of those spots, we'd reach the thousands of families who'd just bought homes. But was that the track God wanted us to follow? My team and I weren't entirely sure.

Around this same time I crossed paths with a couple I had met during my first months at the church, when they were part of New Life's hospitality team. Back then, the husband had come to me to tell me that he and his wife were going to leave New Life to go help a friend of theirs start a church on the south side of town, called Nueva Vida, which coincidentally means "New Life." I was dealing with the immediate and tragic aftermath of the shooting and had my hands full. "I wish I could do more than send you out with my blessing," I explained to him at the time, "but I'm at capacity right now."

The couple left, they and their friend did indeed start Nueva Vida, and God began growing this little congregation in a part of town hungry for spiritual food.

Several years after that initial launch, the senior pastor of that church—this couple's friend—made some poor choices and resigned. The couple asked to meet with me. "Brady," they said, "we just lost our pastor, and at a time when we were beginning to catch our stride. Our congregation has grown to more than one hundred and fifty people, and we have no one to lead us now."

I began meeting more regularly with these two. Since together they'd just taken the senior pastor role, they had lots of questions. We talked about how to create a service-oriented culture in the church; about how to move from one weekend service to two, so that more people could be reached for Christ; and about how to begin setting aside funds so they could move out of their rented space into something more permanent in coming years. Toward the end of one of those training sessions, the husband thanked me for pitching in and then said, "I think it would encourage our congregation if you would come preach for us sometime."

A month later, on a Wednesday night, I found myself sitting in the front row of Nueva Vida next to my then executive pastor, Garvin McCarrell, ready to take the stage. Which is when God nudged me with a prompting that would expand the hearts and minds of our New Life Church. The small choir was singing "Revelation Song" in Spanish as the divine whisper overtook my thoughts, and as the song's chorus rose to the rafters, *"Santo, santo, santo, / Dios todo-Poderoso / Quien fue, quien es, y quien vendra . . .*" I leaned over to Garvin and said, "We're supposed to merge with this church."

When I began plotting chapters for this part of the book, I could think of no better starting point than the subject of race and equality. Based on the grid that I've covered thus far, if I were to strike off as an "instigator" in any one area of life, it would be here, in a ranting, raving, fist-thrust-in-the-air *demand for justice* for every person or group that has ever been marginalized or oppressed. I grew up in the South, where remnants of segregation were everywhere—in my family, in my neighborhood, in my school. Still, I was never able to tolerate the mistreatment of another human being. I had been bullied, as I mentioned before. I knew how it felt to be outcast, to be dehumanized, to be shunned. I wanted no part of that demeaning craziness. I wanted to chart a different course.

I'm sure that this belief is what fueled a later commitment Pam and I made to leave our tiny home in northwest Louisiana every Saturday morning and head over to Abby Street, where I'd "preach" to six elderly women from one front porch or another. Abby Street was featured on the evening news most nights, and the news was never good. Drug busts, murders, raids—it seemed to be pure madness over there. Which is why Pam and I were surprised upon heading over to Abby Street and knocking on doors and forging friendships and looking for ways to spread some resources around to find a completely different side to this part of town, one that never made the ten o'clock news. In addition to being befriended by those six "congregants" of mine, we met dozens of men, women, and children who needed to know that they were seen and valued, that they were loved and protected, that there was hope for them in this life.

As I sat on the front row that night at Nueva Vida, absorbing God's prompting to merge, I nodded in acknowledgment of the truth. *Of course,* I thought as I toyed with the idea. *If we want to serve people in the name of Jesus, why wouldn't we come to where the most needs exist?*

The thought reinforced a long-held belief of mine that if we truly long to emulate Jesus, then we will quit expecting people who have been oppressed to integrate into the culture and structures of their oppressors and the oppressive systems those oppressors have built. Instead, we will leave our comfort, privilege, and convenience and choose to humbly *go to them.* As it related to Nueva Vida, I had no intention of colonizing this church; rather, New Life needed to join forces with them in creating a unified "new." If it worked, it would be remarkable.

I believed in my heart it would work.

Throughout Scripture, we see the through line of God's concern for the poor, the weak, the marginalized, and the oppressed. The prophet Isaiah clearly saw humans being dehumanized, which is what prompted him to call believers to a new approach: "Learn to do good," he wrote in Isaiah 1:17. "Seek justice. Help the oppressed. Defend the cause of orphans. Fight for the rights of widows."

Zechariah wrote: "Do not oppress widows, orphans, foreigners, and the poor. And do not scheme against each other" (Zechariah 7:10). *Don't ignore the issue that's right in front of you,* he might have said. *Don't stand by, refusing to engage.*

Quoting the book of Isaiah, Jesus said of his incarnational arrival, "The Spirit of the LORD is upon me, for he has anointed me to bring Good News to the poor. He has sent me to proclaim that captives will be released, that the blind will see, that the oppressed will be set free, and that the time of the LORD's favor has come" (Luke 4:18–19).

God knew that for captives to truly be set free, he would have to meet them there in their pain and direct them along the path out.

The apostle Paul wrote of this event in his letter to the church at Philippi, saying, "Though he [Jesus] was God, he did not think of equality with God as something to cling to. Instead, he gave up his divine privileges; he took the humble position of a slave and was born as a human being. When he appeared in human form, he humbled himself in obedience to God and died a criminal's death on a cross" (Philippians 2:6–8). Jesus, God the Son, he who is *totally and completely powerful,* humbled himself to come to those who were *totally and completely powerless* and said, in effect, *I see you. I love you. I long to serve your ultimate good.*

But perhaps more staggering than even the event Paul describes is the way that he frames it up. Just before he reminds us of the great lengths that Jesus went to in reaching us, *he tells us to go and do the same.* "You must have the same attitude that Christ Jesus had," verse 5 reads. When we find ourselves in possession of resources and power, in other words, we're to lay down our privilege, humble ourselves, drop our status, and go. And yet, if history has borne out anything, it's that we don't *exactly* like this plan.

In modern times, the most prevalent example of racism and oppression in this country centers on the black experience as far back as our founding. Slavery was a common practice in ancient African and Arab nations before spreading to Europe, and slaves were thought to make up a full 75 percent of the Roman empire by the time Christ arrived on the scene. Closer to home, early Native American tribes practiced slavery as well, only adding to the widespread perception that this tragic practice was an expected and even expedient way of life.

Between the early 1500s and the mid-1800s, the United States received only 7 percent of the ten million African slaves who were deported to the New World, but it was a *very* consequential 7 percent. In the same way that the ancient world had been built on the backs of slaves, including its famous "Seven Wonders"—the Great Pyramid of Giza, the Hanging Gardens of Babylon, the Temple of Artemis, and so forth—all our nation's most prized buildings, including the White House and the U.S. Capitol, were built by the hands of slaves.

At the signing of our Declaration of Independence, which liberated us as a people from English rule, a good percentage of "us" were *anything* but free. That year, 1776, slavery was not just legal but normative in *every one of our fledgling nation's thirteen colonies.*[1] Untangling ourselves from this deeply embedded norm was going to be an uphill climb.

It would take 250 years after British settlers first came ashore in Jamestown for the legal institution of slavery to come to an end. It was 1865, the Civil War had ended, President Lincoln had been assassinated, the Thirteenth Amendment had officially abolished slavery throughout the land, and the final 250,000 slaves, who lived in Texas, finally received word that they were free. But what did this "freedom" really mean?

In 1896 the U.S. Supreme Court ruled that racial segregation was legal as long as the facilities to be used by people who were black were of the same quality as those used by people who were white; "separate but equal," it was named. Slavery may have been ruled illegal, but with segregation quickly taking its place, could black people genuinely feel free? (Incredibly, the court case *Plessy v. Ferguson* still has yet to be officially overruled.)

In 1954, *Brown v. Board of Education* ruled that having separate schools for black and white children was unconstitutional—progress, to be sure, and yet didn't separation still exist? The practice of "redlining" comes to mind, in which financial, real estate, and retail developers draw a boundary around certain zip codes and then systematically deny services to those communities, which are most often made up of minority groups. The trend began in the 1930s and was officially banned in the late 1960s, but remnants of it still persist today.

My point in this little history lesson is this: While the church certainly can't be accused of doing *nothing* in response to these horrific trends, can it rightly be said that we did enough to defend black women and men? Yes, some denominations came out with "statements" standing against racism and its evil ways. Yes, the Southern Baptist Convention denounced the activity of the KKK. But these things hardly represented standing in solidarity with those who had been victimized far too long.

As the ban on segregation formally took hold, Martin Luther King Jr.'s voice could be heard: "Injustice anywhere is a threat to justice everywhere,"[2] he said. Given the posture of the local church, we clearly had work left to do.

Back to that Wednesday night at Nueva Vida. After I preached and Garvin and I wrapped up our conversations with various members of their congregation, we climbed into my truck to head home. We talked earnestly about what such a merger might mean. How would we structure such a financial deal? What kind of leadership support would Nueva Vida require? How would we manage the myriad administrative details? What would our communications plan need to include?

The following weeks included multiple meetings, during which the elders, the executive team, our staff, and various groups within our congregation talked and prayed and planned for the big event. Coincidentally, on the very night that we learned that Donald Trump, a man whose stance on immigration reform is controversial to say the least, had become our nation's forty-fifth president, our elder board met to sign official documentation, stating that Nueva Vida and New Life Church were now one. I was like a kid on Christmas morning the following Sunday as I finalized the remarks I would deliver to our church. But while most of New Life was fully on board with this exciting direction, not everyone was as pleased as I was.

"The largest Hispanic church in our city is now family," I said to New Life during the worship service. "The merger we've been dreaming of? It's a *reality* now." The crowd applauded and stood, even as I knew some in our midst harbored deep concern. After the service, more than a few New Lifers approached to register their complaints. "Most of the members of that congregation are here *illegally*," they protested. "Brady, they've *broken the law*."

Technically, these folks were correct in their assessment. But spiritually I questioned their stance. Hadn't Jesus himself been a heavenly refugee? Hadn't he been marginalized, ostracized, and oppressed? Weren't we as Christ's followers considered pilgrims in this life, waiting to become what the apostle Paul called "citizens of heaven" someday? (See Philippians 3:20.) If anyone could empathize with our Hispanic brothers and sisters who had traveled to a new land, it was us—a people who don't yet feel at home.

To sit with our Christian heritage is to be reminded that we were once the stranger craving warm welcome. We were once the sojourner longing for home. If we claim kinship to "father

Abraham," then we must be willing to claim his status as a refugee—a designation that was handed to him by God. If we desire connection to the "chosen nation" of Israel, then we must be willing to connect to their enslavement, their oppression, their plight. If we wish to associate with Jesus, then we must be willing to associate with the discrimination he suffered while on earth.

Ephesians 2:19 confirms that while believers in Christ indeed have been adopted into God's divine family, we didn't start out that way; we started as "strangers and foreigners" in the land. This historical identity that you and I share—as sojourners, as immigrants, as refugees, as those on the fringes of society looking in—compels us not to *evict* but to *embrace* the strangers in our midst today, knowing that we once were a lot like them.

There were still rumblings of discontent in pockets of our congregation when I got to chapter 9 in the series on 1 Corinthians I was preaching. There the apostle Paul says this: "Even though I am a free man with no master, I have become a slave to all people to bring many to Christ. When I was with the Jews, I lived like a Jew to bring the Jews to Christ. When I was with those who follow the Jewish law, I too lived under that law. Even though I am not subject to the law, I did this so I could bring to Christ those who are under the law. When I am with the Gentiles who do not follow the Jewish law, I too live apart from that law so I can bring them to Christ. But I do not ignore the law of God; I obey the law of Christ.

"When I am with those who are weak, I share their weakness, for I want to bring the weak to Christ. Yes, I try to find common ground with everyone, doing everything I can to save some. I do everything to spread the Good News and share in its blessings" (vv. 19–23).

As I told our congregation that weekend, I believe that the reason those of us who enjoy a fair amount of white privilege today struggle to step outside of our power structures and show up in service to the disempowered in our midst is that we tend to politicize the issues of race and equality, when these aren't political issues at all. The Reverend Martin Luther King Jr. called on believers, not politicians, to put an end to the discrimination he saw. When he started the Southern Christian Leadership Conference in the late 1950s, the organization that would coordinate civil rights activities and protests, he implored its members to mimic the early Christians, who faithfully practiced nonviolence in working to get their point across.[3]

Those of us who live in full surrender to the lordship of Jesus posture ourselves with love, compassion, and empathy toward those who have been mistreated in our midst, not to make a political statement, but to make a human one.

That group of first-century believers may have been small in number, but the quality of their efforts revolutionized the world. This was the group that put a stop to infanticide, the degradation of women, gladiatorial combats, and slavery, to name just a few, and King believed that adopting their same approach would yield similarly significant results. I happen to agree with him here: it is only by the Spirit's power that hearts soften; it is only by the Spirit's power that minds shift; it is only by the Spirit's power that attitudes get rightly adjusted; it is only by the Spirit's power that real progress gets made.

Remember, as Paul's words confirm, the reason we put on weakness in the presence of the weak and enslavement in the presence of the enslaved is for the purpose of *bringing them to Christ* (roman font is my emphasis below).

> *I have become a slave to all people,*
> to bring many to Christ. . . .
> *I lived like a Jew*
> to bring the Jews to Christ. . . .
> *I too lived under that law . . .*
> so I could bring to Christ those under the law.
> *When I am with the Gentiles . . . I too live apart from that law*
> so I can bring them to Christ. . . .
> *I try to find common ground with everyone,*
> doing everything I can to save some.
>
> —1 Corinthians 9:19–23

There's something here we must not miss. Those of us who live in full surrender to the lordship of Jesus posture ourselves with love, compassion, and empathy toward those who have been mistreated in our midst, not to make a political statement, but to make a human one. We do this not because we are witnesses of a voting party but because we're witnesses of the living God. We refuse to hoard our privilege, choosing instead to walk humbly with God and pass the power around.

We live as mouthpieces of Christ's encouraging words. We live as extensions of Christ's outstretched arms. We live as his feet that are eager to serve. We become Jesus' joy, his hope, his liberation, his grace, by staying tender toward *all* those he came to save.

We follow the age-old Golden Rule, treating everyone as we ourselves long to be treated. It shouldn't take something so simple to mark our attitudes and actions as "remarkable," but in fact, such a posture would.

In September 2017 the attorney general of the United States announced on behalf of the president that the administration was thereby ending a program called Deferred Action for Childhood Arrivals, an Obama-era program that protected more than 800,000 undocumented child immigrants to the United States who hailed from Mexico, mostly, but also El Salvador, Guatemala, and Honduras. The announcement promised that the current administration was working to craft "official legislation" that would protect both the country's and these children's best interest, citing the fact that President Obama went around Congress to get DACA approved as a major flaw in the program's efforts.[4] Honestly, that *was* a flaw; when you're dealing with something as tenuous and complex as the handling of immigration, it behooves *any* president to follow protocol. And yet the results were still the results: nearly a million kids who had been living here in a protected state were now thrust into vulnerability unlike any they'd ever known.

In response to the program's repeal, some people—perhaps those of the same mind as the New Lifers who initially protested our Nueva Vida merger—were relieved. They believed that the phrase "illegal immigrant" equated to the phrase "gang-banger" or "drug pusher" or worse. *Finally*, they probably said to themselves, *we'll quit aiding and abetting these thugs.*

These kids weren't thugs. The DACA program *ensured* they weren't thugs.

Had any of those "relieved" folks approached me to solicit support for their side of the story, I would have gently reminded them that DACA had stricter requirements for its program than many middle-class parents have for their kids. To be accepted into DACA's program, a boy or girl had to have come to the United States prior to reaching the sixteenth birthday. The child had to have continuously resided in the United States for five years prior to the date of application. He or she had to be presently enrolled in school, a graduate of high school, or a recipient of a GED. He or she had to have never been convicted of a felony, significant misdemeanor, or three or more "other" misdemeanors. He or she had to pose no threat to national security or public safety. He or she had to have never been arrested or charged with any criminal convictions. And he or she had to pay a steep application fee just to get the process under way. Again: these were not thugs. These were boys and girls who had lived in this country for the bulk of their growing-up years and only would have felt like "immigrants" had we sent them back to their parents' hometown.[5]

Once approved, "DACA kids" would receive valid driver's licenses, permission to enroll in college, and the ability to legally get a job. As legal employees, they would be asked to pay income tax.[6]

The DACA program didn't provide a means for these kids to become legal citizens or even permanent residents; it simply provided a two-year holding pattern until further legislation was made.

Now, here's why I bring all of this up: given the journey with Nueva Vida that we as a church had been on, when news of this turn of events hit, what normally would have been solely a political discussion never mentioned politics once. When New Lifers came up to me around town or following services or via email, the comments revolved around "our kids." Many of "our kids" at Nueva Vida had been protected by DACA. It was "our kids" who were vulnerable now. "Our kids" might face deportation. "Our kids" needed help—and fast. Across the time that had passed between the merger and DACA's repeal, New Lifers had gone to worship with Nueva Vida, and Nueva Vida's members had come to worship with us. "Illegal immigrants" and "privileged white folk" suddenly had real faces, real names, real families, real children, real lives. We learned each other's stories as those weeks gave way to months. We found common ground on which all our feet could stand. We shared laughter and hopes, meals and dreams; in the end we became true friends. And so, when this country decided that the provisions that had been afforded to so many children would be suddenly rendered null and void, friends behaved as you'd expect friends to behave. We came alongside. We *cared*. It was a remarkable moment, I must say.

In 1 Corinthians 12, the apostle Paul described how the body of Christ is like that of a human: "Many parts make up one whole body." Some are "Jews," he wrote, "some are Gentiles, some are slaves, and some are free. But we all have been baptized into one body by one Spirit, and we all share the same Spirit" (vv. 12–13). Paul went on to talk about how a foot was no less a part of the body because it wasn't a hand, and how an ear was no less a part of the body because it wasn't an eye. I couldn't help but think of that passage as I watched our churches meld. We needed each other, plain and simple. Nueva Vida families needed advocates, and New Lifers needed a reality check. Life was *challenging* to those without privilege. This power we held? It needed to *spread.*

Listen, on this issue of humanizing our fellow humans, only time will tell of what will happen as believers wake up and start to care. I don't know what program will replace DACA; I don't know what our Congress will do. But this much I do know: as you and I assume our role of being not political advocates but rather *prophetic voices speaking truth to our politicians,* important stuff will finally get done.

"Christians have a vital role in making sure that the needs of refugees are taken seriously by national governments," wrote Christine D. Pohl, in her book *Making Room: Recovering Hospitality as a Christian Tradition.* "But our response must extend beyond public policy to more personal involvement in voluntary agencies, communities, churches, and homes where acts of welcome offer refuge and new life to some of the world's most vulnerable people."[7] *This* is where progress begins. As Pastor Charlie Dates said in his national speech commemorating the fiftieth anniversary of the death of Martin Luther King Jr., *apologies* are nice from those who have perpetuated discrimination down through the ages, but *strategies* are better. It is high time to strategize. I believe in the benefits of an orderly system. I believe in the rule of law. I believe that our borders must be protected. I believe that our government officials should be trusted to do their jobs. But here is what I also believe: I believe that until we as a people come up with *compassionate legislation* that allows those who come to our nation, adhere to stringent standards, and add beautiful value to our culture to *flourish here over the long haul,* our work is far from done.

So. What to do now? I want to invite you into the practices that many from our church have been engaging in in their quest to quit being part of the problem and start being part of the solution. To stand by is no longer an option; today is the day to act—not according to your own will and ways but according to those of God. In preparation for his prompting, may you and I both:

Get an attitude check. Consider searching your heart before the Lord to see where pockets of discrimination might reside. Check for complacency. Check for self-absorption. Check for hesitancy. Check for fear. Do you walk through life with an air of superiority? Do you think "those people" are less than or wrong? Are you exclusive? Are you closed off? Or are you *welcoming toward one and all*?

Ask yourself, *When was the last time I engaged someone in conversation who looked and acted* nothing *like me?*

Ask, *Is there a place at my table for people who are different from me, or do I only engage those who are same, same, same?*

Ask, *Is there room in my belief system for strangers who long to call this country home, or will I spend a lifetime protesting their rule-breaking ways and neglecting them Jesus' great care?*

Paul's words in Galatians 3:28 remind us that in Christ "there is no longer Jew or Gentile, slave or free, male and female," and certainly the list could go on. There is no longer black or white. There is no longer immigrant or citizen. There is no longer old or young. There is no longer rich or poor. In our current context, we might add: there is no longer gay and straight; there is no longer user of weed and abstainer of weed; there is no longer conservative and progressive. In Jesus, we all are one; while we will never (and must never!) lose our distinctiveness, the only *dividing lines* in existence are the ones we ourselves choose to draw.

Get educated. Speaking as a fellow social media enthusiast, may I implore us both to seek out information on these critical topics that isn't conveyed in four lines or less?

If you are just beginning to explore the subjects of race and equality in our day, consider checking out Matthew Soerens and Jenny Yang's *Welcoming the Stranger: Justice, Compassion & Truth in the Immigration Debate*; Austin Channing Brown's *I'm Still Here: Black Dignity in a World Made for Whiteness*; the Christian Community Development Association (ccda.org); Neighborly Faith (neighborlyfaith.org); or the work of the Evangelical Immigration Table (evangelicalimmigrationtable.org).

So much of discriminatory behavior comes down to plain old fear, and yet surrendering to this emotion is antithetical to the way of Christ. We have not been given "a spirit of fear and timidity," according to 2 Timothy 1:7, "but of power, love, and self-discipline." Some translations refer to that last benefit as "a sound mind." I find that educating myself on key issues contributes *greatly* to soundness of mind.

Get involved. One of my favorite ministry moments of the past month happened on a Saturday morning at New Life when our church hosted Senator (formerly Representative) Tim Scott, a black man, and Congressman Trey Gowdy, a white man, for a discussion on unity. Tim and Trey are both from South Carolina and met when they were elected to the United States Congress in November 2010. Their friendship initially was formed by their mutual love for the Dallas Cowboys and the South Carolina Gamecocks, but eventually conversations went deep. Political life was challenging. Commuting between Carolina and D.C. was grueling. Stresses in life were mounting. They both needed an earnest friend.

There were four freshman congressmen from South Carolina that year, and given their shared experience the men began meeting for weekly dinners—same restaurant, same table, same night. But as so often is the case, other obligations tugged on their time and, for two of them, eventually won out. Tim and Trey were the two guys left. Week after week they showed up. They opened up. And they grew in their understanding of each other.

Before several hundred members of our congregation on that Saturday morning, Trey helped to illuminate the persisting issue of racism in our country, explaining to those of us who grew up in privilege that not everyone's experience goes like ours. He told the story of having worked in the U.S. attorney general's office in the late 1990s, and how at that time, a person found to be in possession of five hundred grams of powder cocaine would automatically be sentenced to a mandatory five-year prison sentence. It didn't matter what color your skin was: if you were caught with five hundred grams of powder cocaine, you'd go to prison for five years.

At the same time, another law was on the books. If a person—regardless of race—was found to be in possession of five grams of cocaine base, also called crack cocaine, the same mandatory five-year sentence was enforced.

"As far as the law was concerned," Trey said, "all was fair. But in terms of the *application* of the law, it wasn't fair at all. Guess whose drug of choice historically has been powder cocaine? People who are white. Guess whose drug of choice is crack? People who are black."[8]

Granted, the Fair Sentencing Act of 2010 helped even things out, but only slightly, bringing the disparity ratio down from 100:1 to 18:1. There is still plenty of work to be done.

Tim then recounted the night he learned of the tragic shooting in his home state at Emanuel African Methodist Episcopal Church. "Fifty years ago," Tim said, "I couldn't have been friends with a guy like Trey. We couldn't have graduated from the same schools, we couldn't have eaten at the same restaurants, and we couldn't have drunk from the same water fountains. And yet on that night in July 2015, when I learned of a racially charged mass murder by a self-proclaimed white supremacist that had unfolded in my state in the church where my uncle had worshipped for five decades, who did I turn to for comfort? A middle-age white guy, Trey Gowdy. We're not where we need to be as a country, but *that* is a sign of progress."

Tim is right. We do have a long way to go in dismantling structures of evil and dispersing power in this country beyond the white male, but we mustn't underestimate the beauty that can unfold from opening ourselves to real relationships with those who are unlike us. In my own life, as I've been working to deepen my friendships with the black and brown pastors, congregants, and friends I know and respect, simply picking up the phone on the heels of a race-related current event and saying, "Help me understand your perspective on this: What am I missing here?" has gone a long way in fostering shared understanding and growth.

Tell me your story . . .

Help me understand . . .

Give me your perspective . . .

I'd love to know more . . .

Openers such as these indicate the posture of humility and teachability we'd all do better to hold. When you and I devote ourselves to actively restoring humanity to *all* human beings—migrant workers, LGBTQ persons, Muslims, black teenagers, women . . . *all* who have been systemically oppressed—the lines that have divided us will get erased. And then is when things get interesting. *Then* is when we live out God's dream.

Most weekends at New Life, we end our worship service by taking communion together—and, to be candid, it's the best part of the whole deal. Our musicians work hard to craft powerful experiences with song. Our pastoral staff works hard to invite the congregation into times of meaningful prayer and ministry. The other teaching pastors and I work hard to put together impactful messages that prompt people to deeper intimacy with Jesus. And I haven't even gotten to the children's workers and parking lot greeters and volunteers and ushers and more. My point is that all of us treat these various aspects of ministry with reverence and respect. But if you were to tell me that I could keep only one element of the worship service and that everything else had to go away, I would hold fast to our time at the Lord's table, where we are all distinctly one.

In the book of Revelation, John is given a divine vision of the reality believers will one day enjoy. He wrote:

> *After this [the preservation of God's people] I saw a vast crowd, too great to count, from every nation and tribe and people and language, standing in front of the throne before the Lamb. They were clothed in white robes and held palm branches in their hands. And they were shouting with a great roar, "Salvation comes from our God who sits on the throne and from the Lamb!"*
>
> *And all the angels were standing around the throne and around the elders and the four living beings. And they fell before the throne with their faces to the ground and worshiped*

God. They sang, "Amen! Blessing and glory and wisdom and thanksgiving and honor and power and strength belong to our God forever and ever! Amen."

Then one of the twenty-four elders asked me, "Who are these who are clothed in white? Where did they come from?"

And I said to him, "Sir, you are the one who knows."

Then he said to me, "These are the ones who died in the great tribulation. They have washed their robes in the blood of the Lamb and made them white.

"That is why they stand in front of God's throne and serve him day and night in his Temple. And he who sits on the throne will give them shelter. They will never again be hungry or thirsty; they will never be scorched by the heat of the sun. For the Lamb on the throne will be their Shepherd. He will lead them to springs of life-giving water. And God will wipe every tear from their eyes [Revelation 7:9–17].

Each weekend, when I watch thousands of people stream down the aisles toward the dozen or so communion stations to pick up the bread and cup, I think about that scene involving those from *every* nation, from *every* tribe, from *every* people, from *every* language, and I get choked up every time. Women and men and rich and poor and black and white and natives and immigrants and old and young and officers of the law and those who broke the law just last night . . . here they *all* are, worshipping God.

You know, back in our text from Paul to the Corinthians, the apostle rebuked the church for treating communion lightly, saying, "When you meet together, you are not really interested in the Lord's Supper. For some of you hurry to eat your own meal without sharing with others. As a result, some go hungry while others get drunk. What? Don't you have your own homes for eating and drinking? Or do you really want to disgrace God's church and shame the poor? What am I supposed to say? Do you want me to praise you? Well, I certainly will not praise you for this!" (1 Corinthians 11:20–22).

Paul then reminds the believers who were gathered there—and also us—what the meaning of communion truly is. "For I pass on to you what I received from the Lord himself," he wrote. "On the night when he was betrayed, the Lord Jesus took some bread and gave thanks to God for it. Then he broke it in pieces and said, 'This is my body, which is given for you. Do this in remembrance of me.' In the same way, he took the cup of wine after supper, saying, 'This cup is the new covenant between God and his people—an agreement confirmed with my blood. Do this in remembrance of me as often as you drink it.' For every time you eat this bread and drink this cup, you are announcing the Lord's death until he comes again" (vv. 23–26).

The final exhortation Paul offers the church is the most powerful one, in my view. In verse 33 he says, "So, my dear brothers and sisters, when you gather for the Lord's Supper, *wait for each other*. If you are really hungry, eat at home so you won't bring judgment upon yourselves when you meet together. I'll give you instructions about the other matters after I arrive" (vv. 33–34, emphasis mine). That little phrase "wait for each other"—don't miss the power of those words.

In the immediate context of communion, yes, we are to wait until everyone has been given the elements before partaking of the bread and cup. But I can't help but imagine a broader application of the phrase, a grander *waiting for each other* taking place. I see a reality in which each person created in the image of God—regardless of color, creed, gender, socioeconomic status, or citizenship—is *waited on* by everyone else. There is no imbalance in power, because power is enjoyed by all. There is no disproportion in privilege, because privilege is enjoyed by all. There is no inequality in rights, because rights are enjoyed by all. By the power of Jesus living inside of us, we really can help usher in the day when no one is made to suffer oppression at another's hand. On that day there really will be no more hunger. There really will be no more thirst. There really will be no more scorching enslavement. *Freedom* will have its way. And that freedom we say we long for, not just for ourselves but for *all* humankind? It comes only when we choose to wait for each other.

I see a reality in which each person created in the image of God—regardless of color, creed, gender, socioeconomic status, or citizenship—is *waited on* by everyone else.

We wait for each other because we belong to each other. I'm yours. And, remarkably, you are mine.

5

The Opposite of Condemnation

We Can Reflect Remarkable Grace

I wish grace and healing were more abracadabra kind of things . . . But no, it's clog and slog and scootch, on the floor, in silence, in the dark.

ANNE LAMOTT

I know something about you, and it's not one of the more flattering aspects of your life. Even if you and I have never met, even if I don't know the ins and outs of your story, even if I don't know your name or where you're from or who your family members are or what you do for a living or what sports teams you root for or how you spend your time and energy and money in a given month—even if I know *none* of these things—there is one thing I definitely know, and it is this: *You have a scandalous past.*

You can protest and hedge and explain and defend, and yet what I'm saying is still totally true: you—no matter who you are, what you've done, what you *haven't* done, and when those doings and not-doings might have occurred—have a scandalous past.

I know this because I, too, have a scandalous past. In fact, every person who has ever lived and every person who will call earth home in years to come—we all share a common past. And that past is utterly scandalous, thanks to our forebears, a garden, and some fruit.

You know this story well. God created the universe and stars and plants and creatures to creep on the ground and then, for his big finale, he created humankind. The crown of all creation, it was deemed, intricate, beautiful, *good*. God set up the debut couple, Adam and Eve, in the Garden of Eden, where they were told to tend and watch over all living things. "You may freely eat the fruit of every tree in the garden," God instructed Adam, in what amounted to the singular rule of the place, "except the tree of the knowledge of good and evil" (Genesis 2:16–17). There would be certain punishment for breaking this rule, God explained, saying that if Adam ate that tree's fruit, he would "surely die" (v. 17, KJV). Adam heard the rule. He understood the rule. And then he proceeded to break it, with Eve playing no small role. And indeed, just as God had foretold, something precious in that couple ceased to exist.

Where they had once enjoyed unrushed, unencumbered communion with their heavenly Father, they'd now been evicted from that place. Where they had once enjoyed complete candor with each other and with God, they now hid. Where they had once enjoyed life as it was meant to be lived, they now knew brokenness and deep pain. Their story is our story; their past is our past; their scandal is our scandal. This is our heritage, yours and mine. This is what's true of us. We've all heard the rule and understood the rule and then in a bout of self-centered stubbornness broken that rule we heard and understood. We've all experienced the certain death that occurs whenever we abandon God's way for our own.

And yet this is hardly the sum of our story, right? The separation and ostracism and embarrassment and grief that always accompany waywardness thankfully did not win the day. Eventually there would be wholeness. Eventually there would be peace. Eventually there would be communion. Eventually we'd be *redeemed*. Because of God's marvelous gift of grace in our lives, all would be made new.

I know something else about you.

Even if you and I have never met, this much I know: If you're a follower of Christ's, then you are *not who you once were*. You are a completely remade creation, says Galatians 2:20, now awake, alive in Christ.

If you're like me, then you remember the day you encountered grace, the day you were given fresh identity, fresh purpose, fresh air. No more running. No more hiding. No more striving. No more fear. Undeserved favor had finally found you. At last you'd begin again. Whatever you'd been before that day—scoundrel, sinner, rebel, crook—your name now was *child*.

Beloved daughter.

Beloved son.

Cherished co-laborer.

Friend.

That day felt *incredible*, didn't it?

I was twenty-one years old before I fully "grasped" grace. I'd stubbornly wedged myself in a dark tunnel for the handful of years prior, determined to go my own way, but in the end, God's grace was too compelling for me. I simply no longer could choose to resist. That, and my mom was determined that I know God. During that extended season of teenage rebellion, I would stumble home, only marginally sober, and crash into bed, clothes still on. I'd get a few hours of sleep before the same loud voice woke me. It was Mom. Again. Praying to God. For me. She neither judged me nor condemned me in those prayers, despite her having every reason to do so. Instead, she prayed earnestly that I would come to Jesus and love him and live for him all my days.

My mother knew what it was to go one's own way in life. She'd grown up hearing horror stories about her history, her heritage, her past. The reason she was raising her kids in northern Louisiana in the first place was because her great-great-grandfather had killed a federal agent and was on the run. He'd settled in the backwoods of Louisiana, believing that there he'd be safe, and while he was indeed able to escape the law, he couldn't escape the murderous legacy he'd left. By the time I showed up in 1967, my family had been living in the same small town for seventy-seven years, and only now, with my mom and dad's influence, did our family name mean something *other* than criminal, fugitive, and the like. My dad said what he meant and meant what he said, and he taught my siblings and me to do the same. He and my mom were hard workers who earned an honest wage and served their community well. When my mom finally saw the suspicion lift from the community's perception regarding who she was and where she'd come from, it was like she was breathing clean oxygen for the first time. Our name meant something to them, and at last that something was *good.* She didn't want me to go and screw that up.

On that August night in 1988 when I finally surrendered myself fully to Christ, I understood what my mom meant. The name "Christian," for all the current-day baggage it bears, meant something profoundly beautiful to me. Despite my family's past, and despite my own past, for me, *all things were made new*. Grace had paved the way for me to come close to God; it was grace that had made me new. Ephesians 2:8 says it this way: "God saved you by his grace when you believed. And you can't take credit for this; it is a gift from God."

God chose to lavish us with grace so that our grace-drenched lives would point people back to him. It was a terrific plan, you probably agree, even as down through the ages, lovers of God have refused to let it play out.

When the apostle Paul came to the believers who were gathered at Corinth, he wasted no time in addressing the heart of the problems he saw. Yes, he saw how they had assimilated into Corinthian culture, which prized pleasures that were temporal at best. But this was mere window dressing compared with the cracks in the foundation Paul found. "I appeal to you, dear brothers and sisters," he wrote, "by the authority of our Lord Jesus Christ, to *live in harmony with each other*. Let there be no divisions in the church. Rather, be of one mind, united in thought and purpose" (1 Corinthians 1:10, emphasis mine).

Paul went on to detail the rumors he'd heard—of the infighting, the quarrels, the pain—and you get the sense from the urgency of his message that he was more than ready for these patterns to stop.

"If you have legal disputes about such matters, why go to outside judges who are not respected by the church? I am saying this to shame you. Isn't there anyone in all the church who is wise enough to decide these issues? But instead, one believer sues another—right in front of unbelievers!

"Even to have such lawsuits with one another is a defeat for you. Why not just accept the injustice and leave it at that? Why not let yourselves be cheated? Instead, you yourselves are the ones who do wrong and cheat even your fellow believers" (1 Corinthians 6:4–8).

Now, it would be nice if we could hang this input of Paul's solely on the matter at hand: *lawsuits*. It would be nice to say to ourselves, *Got it. As long as I don't sue another believer, I'm good*. But of course the implications are far broader than that.

You and I are building something important here, Paul was saying to the Corinthians. *And the foundation on which we build is grace*. His point was that we must be extremely careful about what we choose to put atop that pristine foundation, because that which is incongruent with grace will not survive God's judgment in the end. "Anyone who builds on that foundation may use a variety of materials—gold, silver, jewels, wood, hay, or straw," Paul wrote. "But on that judgment day, fire will reveal what kind of work each builder has done. The fire will show if a person's work has any value. If the work survives, that builder will receive a reward. But if the work is burned up, the builder will suffer great loss. The builder will be saved, but like someone barely escaping through a wall of flames.

"Don't you realize that all of you together are the temple of God and that the Spirit of God lives in you? God will destroy anyone who destroys this temple. For God's temple is holy, and you are that temple" (1 Corinthians 3:12–17). And so:

Quit fighting with each other!
Quit killing unity within the church!
Quit fussin'! as we'd say in the South.

To fuss is to gripe. To agitate. To mess with. It's not always an outright fight, mind you; sometimes it's just *stirring something up*.

The point is, to stir something up is the opposite of settling something down, of bringing a sense of calm to an environment, of ushering in much-needed peace. Pam and I spent time with a family from Texas recently, and I couldn't help but notice that whenever the dad was in the room, the three sons, all of whom were teenagers, seemed more at ease. They were good kids to begin with, but the closer their father came to them, the more their countenance relaxed. Their dad was a *blessing* to them. He was a stabilizer. He was a bearer of beautiful peace. That's the picture Paul was promoting to the Corinthian church. *Bring stability!* he was saying. *Bring calmness!* Bring grace.

Paul's reminder to the Corinthians was necessary for the same reason it's necessary for us. How will we compel those outside the faith to consider Christ when we can't get along with those already here? Plainly stated, *we are no help to a world in need of grace unless such graciousness marks our lives.* The greatest temptation for you and me, upon devoting our lives to Christ, is not pride or rebellion or lust or greed, as powerful as each of those is. No, the greatest temptation is simple *forgetfulness*. We forget who we were before grace.

Paul referenced the "work" that each of us is responsible for, that thing we choose to lay on God's foundation of grace. For the balance of this chapter, I'd like to look at three practices that lead to laudable work, three "grace endeavors" that are congruent with the foundation God has laid for our lives. They are these: acceptance, kindness, and forgiveness—the trifecta of a gracious life.

PRACTICE 1: ACCEPTANCE

In Western culture, which prizes pulling ourselves up by our bootstraps and dealing with life on our own, we don't quite know what to do with grace. We can't earn it, or it is no longer a free gift. We can't strive for it, or it is no longer simply received. We can't claim it as our own, or it is no longer divinely handed to us. No, to experience God's grace, we must just *come*—hands empty, hearts open, minds blown. We must acknowledge that no amount of human winsomeness, wisdom, or wit will accomplish that which we desperately need accomplished: namely, a reset of our entire lives—body, mind, soul. And then, perhaps more pressing still, we must stay in touch with that reset we gained.

You're probably familiar with the parable of the Good Samaritan. To refresh your memory, as the story goes, a man is robbed while making his way from one town to another. He is thrown into a ditch by the robbers, where he lies, beaten and bloody, waiting for help. Religious leaders happen by but, despite the high value they place on moral living, they do not stop. The man in the ditch is unclean, and to touch an unclean person in those days would be to disqualify oneself from entering the temple to worship God. The religious leaders needed to get to the temple, they reasoned, which meant that of course they could not stop.

Soon after the religious leaders departed, another man approached, this one from the region of Samaria. Now, in this culture, Samaritans were considered by Jews to be a suspicious lot, ostracized for what were considered deviant ways of worshipping God. They were looked down upon and avoided in much the same way that some evangelicals look down on and avoid Palestinians, Muslims, and liberal Christians. And yet here a Samaritan man comes close to the one who had been robbed and beaten, and he offers a helping hand.

The Good Samaritan knew how awful it felt to be mistreated, misunderstood, cast aside. And so his reflexive response to finding another in need was to stop what he was doing and help. In the parable that Jesus told his disciples that day, the perceived "heretic" was presented as the hero—the Jews' "enemy" was the one who'd gotten it right. Not only had this suspicious Samaritan stopped what he was doing to help, but he then lingered to be sure the man was okay. He picked him up, loaded him onto his donkey, and transported him to the nearest inn, where that man was invited to stay the night and eat and rest, all at the Samaritan's expense. Such generosity. Such thoughtfulness. Such grace. And I struggle to keep my cool when the barista at Starbucks takes too long.

You and I were given oceans upon oceans of grace from our heavenly Father. Might we spare an ocean ourselves?

A decade or so ago, a research study made quite a splash that detailed how young people viewed evangelical Christianity. Their view was less than favorable, to say the least: of the top twelve perceptions they held regarding what they considered to be the "faith of their parents," nine of them were negative in tone. For starters, they believed evangelical Christians were too involved in politics (75 percent), too old-fashioned (78 percent), and hypocritical (85 percent). They had strong opinions as well on how their parents' generation treated people who were gay. But the perception that topped the list—the one word that was cited more than any other in terms of how young people viewed evangelical Christians—was this one: "judgmental."[1] They believed that Christians spent way too much time and energy *condemning* others instead of graciously welcoming them in. Looking back at the parable of the Good Samaritan, those surveyed saw evangelical Christians as the religious leaders who sauntered by instead of as the Samaritan who stopped to help—which, if you're an evangelical Christian, as I am, is a real problem for you and me.

In Matthew 7:1–5, Jesus doesn't mince words regarding the posture of acceptance he expects his followers to have. "Do not judge others," he says, "and you will not be judged. For you will be treated as you treat others. The standard you use in judging is the standard by which you will be judged.

"And why worry about a speck in your friend's eye when you have a log in your own? How can you think of saying to your friend, 'Let me help you get rid of that speck in your eye,' when you can't see past the log in your own eye? Hypocrite! First get rid of the log in your own eye; then you will see well enough to deal with the speck in your friend's eye."

Go ahead and refuse to accept people who are unlike you, Jesus implies, but remember: that judgment will come back to you. The point is this: whenever you and I refuse to graciously accept another person—whether because of that person's gender, background, nationality, race, religion, sexual preference, socioeconomic status, appearance, accent, voting record, hygiene habits, or any of a thousand other distinctions—we are essentially saying to God and to that person: *The divine life preserver that was tossed to me, when I was adrift at sea, isn't strong enough to hold you. I'm sorry, but you're on your own.*

Now, I would be remiss if I didn't acknowledge that on a parallel track to Jesus' expectation that you and I graciously accept all people is his expectation that we use caution in determining who we'll go deeper with, who we'll call a beloved friend. We see a progression in the story of Jesus ministering to the adulterous woman that is important not to miss. Jesus had returned to the Mount of Olives and was teaching at the temple, when a crowd gathered nearby. As he spoke, a group of religious leaders brought a woman before him who had been caught in adultery.

"Teacher," they said to Jesus, "this woman was caught in the act of adultery. The law of Moses says to stone her. What do you say?" (John 8:4–5).

Judge her! those leaders were in effect imploring Jesus, in what verse 6 says was a trap. *Put her in her place!*

Jesus famously crouched down to write something in the sand with his finger, as the leaders demanded a response. At last he rises. He says, "All right, but let the one who has never sinned throw the first stone" (v. 7). This was another take on his *Take the log out of your own eye before removing the speck from another's* approach to winning friends and influencing people, and as expected, those leaders dropped their stones. But that's not where the story ends. After Jesus confirms with this woman that not only have her accusers all fled the scene but also that he does not condemn her, he says these critical words: "Go and sin no more" (v. 11).

Jesus delivered this message lovingly. He delivered it thoughtfully. He delivered it with compassion. But he said what needed to be said: "Go and sin no more." He'd accepted her. He'd defended her. He'd conveyed warmth and gentleness and grace. But he'd also called her to a higher level of living, to life that was truly life. We must not miss this vital progression. This is grace at work in the world.

I'm often asked by well-intentioned churchgoers how they're supposed to accept people who are so blatantly sinning against God. They point to the coworker who is cheating on her spouse, or to the young adult who won't get out of their basement and get a job, or to the boss who is considered a misogynist, and with incredulity ask, "How am I supposed to accept *that*?"

I understand their point. Really, I do. Most of us are struggling enough as it is to put off the things that entangle us and run this race effectively. To voluntarily embrace unrighteousness seems like a perilous choice to make. But here's what I want to tell you: *our acceptance need not be blind.*

Around the time that Abram and Callie hit double digits, I remember them feeling emboldened to start picking their own friends. When our kids are young, we tend to steer them toward friendships we believe are safe for them, toward families that are known entities to us. But as years go by and maturity takes root, our children take on that responsibility for themselves. It was then that I clarified for them the difference between "judging" and "evaluating."

"As your dad," I told my kids, "I commit to being nonjudgmental regarding your friends. But you'd better believe I will be *evaluating* the boys and girls you're hanging around. From here on out, 'Assessment' is my middle name."

We can't be "as shrewd as snakes and as innocent as doves," as Jesus instructs his followers in Matthew 10:16 (NIV), unless we thoughtfully, intentionally *do both.* And to be as shrewd as snakes requires that we *engage*, not that we blindly accept whatever this world throws our way. So, yes: as we approach the culture in which we live, may our smiles and hearts and arms be opened wide. May we accept all people, as the image bearers of God that they are. May we exude graciousness at every turn, remembering that we, too, were lavished with grace. And may we radiate the warmth and compassion of Jesus, who once took in our messiest messiness and said, "You are welcome here."

And.

May we also practice careful evaluation of those in our midst, so that we are not led astray.

Did you know that it's possible to take in a teenager who is making really bad choices and express *concern* without getting mad? Did you know that it's possible to interact with someone who votes for a different political party and express warmth instead of pride? Did you know that it's possible to project the countenance *I sure would love to serve you* instead of *Stay away from me!*?

We can live this way—truly we can. We can hold civil conversations without giving up our convictions. We can enfold in community people who are different from us. We can dole out grace by the bucketful, giving lavishly that which we have received. We can, as the apostle Paul said to the church at Corinth, accept all and love all, and get this graciousness thing straight now so that "we won't have to be straightened out later on" (1 Corinthians 11:31, MSG).

PRACTICE 2: **KINDNESS**

Accepting each other is but the first step in adopting a gracious posture in this world; once we've accepted another, quite naturally, we'll need to engage. The question that arises, then, is how kind will we be?

The cover photo on my Facebook account is of Pam and me with our kids. We are walking in New York City, which is a favorite travel destination of ours, on Fifty-Sixth Street in Midtown. Now, if you looked at that photo and had nothing else to go on, you'd think we were the perfect family: walking in lockstep, all smiles, enjoying a vacation together in the Big Apple. The truth is that a few hours before that photo was taken, I was *really* ugly to Pam.

One of the strengths of my wife is her steadiness. She is about as unflappable as they come: even-keeled, easygoing, steady nearly all the time. These are all marvelous qualities for a person to have, except for when we're running late. Pam has but one gear, and that gear does not account for those times when we need to rush. "Hustle" isn't exactly in Pam's repertoire. She is measured. Thoughtful. Deliberate.

On most days I find this lack of hurriedness to be a blessing. But on certain occasions—such as ones that involve unexpected traffic, an airport, and a flight about to take off—I wish my wife would share my stress, kick things up a notch, and *go*.

Which brings me to Denver Airport, where we were to catch our flight to New York. Upon seeing the flood of passengers waiting to get through the security line and realizing that unless we hurried up we would, in fact, miss our flight, I turned to Pam, who was lagging a bit behind, and said something along the lines of "Let's go! *Now!* Keep up!"

Only after we were successfully at the gate, preparing to board the flight that we did not miss, did I realize how deeply

I'd hurt my wife. She'd been stung by my words, my lack of kindness, and her look told me I'd been a fool.

I see that picture every time I log onto Facebook, and I can't help but wince. But I leave it there to remind me what I'm capable of: apart from the moment-by-moment welcoming of the Holy Spirit's activity in my life, I'm not that nice of a guy.

In our quest to become more gracious, we must remember to be consistently kind. You can't *imagine* how far a gentle word—a tender touch, a loving response—can take you. You want to be considered remarkably gracious? I'm telling you: *kindness* is the path for you. Start choosing kindness when you'd be justified to fire back or pounce, and you'll set yourself beautifully apart.

I look back on that exchange with Pam and wish I could try again. I wish I could choose to manifest *kindness* to her, even if it meant missing our flight.

"For God's temple is holy, and you are that temple"—the words of 1 Corinthians 3:17 come to mind just now, words that beg the question: How "holy" do you think I was, there at Denver Airport, as I snapped mercilessly at my wife? How much of the Spirit of God do you think Pam saw in me in that moment? Furthermore, how likely do you think it would have been that someone who was making choices in life that hurt himself and/or others would have seen my little display and said to him- or herself, *Wow, I am so impressed by that man's attitude and actions that I simply* must *ask him how he's able to live such a noble and upright life*?

I'll go out on a limb here and say: not very likely at all.

In that split second of neglect, we abandon the holiness

God has asked us to prize. What a horrible way to move through life, doing the opposite of what God said to do. And so, if you need to shore up your habits a little as you represent the Spirit of God to a watching world, try these ideas on for size:

- *Slow down.* Very little good happens as we crazily run around. (Thank you, Pam.)
- *Plug in.* For several years now I have begun each day with a simple prayer: *Come, Holy Spirit.* His power is greater than my power; I do well to plug in to him. Often, I'll ask a rhetorical question as I prepare to engage with another human being: *What would change about this interaction, if I invited the Spirit to take control?* If you're ready for kindness to have its way in your life, I dare you to give that a try . . .
- *Pray now.* And finally, pray, pray, pray, pray, pray. Some people equate kindness with weakness, but I find the opposite is true. In my experience, it takes vastly more self-control to be kind than to be abrupt. Kindness requires that I consider my natural instincts and self-seeking impulses and *choose to take another tack*; if you think *that* doesn't take some serious divine strength, then you're probably also able to walk by a tray of hot, fresh donuts en route to the produce department. (I can like you, but I can't be like you. I'm going to need some baked goods. Baked goods and prayer.) Prayer for wisdom, prayer for insight, prayer for patience, prayer for gentleness, prayer for humility, prayer for the attain-

ment of a timely word, prayer for self-control. Ask, the Bible clearly states, and when that asking is in accordance with God's will, you shall receive.

PRACTICE 3: **FORGIVENESS**

A third manifestation of graciousness is this: *forgiveness*. Forgiveness is a curious thing. We tend to cheer for those who display a forgiving spirit, even as we have trouble following suit. I mentioned the horrific church shooting in Charleston earlier, when a man with racist motivations opened fire at a Wednesday evening prayer meeting, killing nine people, including the church's senior pastor, Clementa Pinckney. The man, a twenty-one-year-old white supremacist, actually sat through that entire prayer meeting listening to the petitions and prayers of the faithful thirteen Christ followers in attendance before standing up, pulling a gun from his fanny pack, and pulling the trigger on men, women, and children in the room. "You want something to pray about?" he reportedly said. "I'll give you something to pray about!"[2]

Two days after that shooting, the gunman made his first court appearance, where the judge was to set his bond. One by one, representatives of the families of each of the victims stood to address the shooter, who appeared by video feed from a heavily guarded holding cell. And one by one those family members forgave the person who had taken their loved ones' lives.

"I forgive you," victim Ethel Lance's daughter said to the

gunman. "I will never be able to hold her [Ethel] again, but I forgive you . . . If God forgives you, I forgive you."

Victim DePayne Middleton Doctor's sister said, "I acknowledge that I'm very angry . . . [But we] have no room for hating, so we have to forgive. I pray God on your soul."[3]

It was a powerful thing, hearing words of gracious forgiveness spoken at a time when rage would have made sense. I was moved by that display, as was anyone in this country with a heart. Forgiveness proves that God is still at work in this world, growing us up, helping us thrive, changing us for the good.

Two years ago I sustained a tough relational blow. A friend of several years and I were suddenly and dramatically on the outs. I had tried everything I could think of to reconcile the situation, but my attempts were all in vain. Eighteen months passed with no words between us . . . Such a strong connection we'd enjoyed, and then *poof*—it was gone. I still loved this person. I still cared for this person. I still longed to call this person my friend. And yet it had become clear to me that by continuing to reach out when he clearly didn't wish to engage might make an already tenuous situation far worse.

At about month nineteen, I was standing in my flower garden in front of my house, picking weeds and watering plants, when my phone rang. Gardening is cheap therapy for me, and I find that the neater my yard looks, the neater my inner world tends to be. However, gardening therapy is hard work in Colorado: You can stick a perennial in the ground and expect it to do well for about a year, but it probably will not come back. Our soil is terrible, our winters can be long and harsh, and outdoor miracles are rarely seen. I remember thinking, *Why am I wasting precious water on this pile of shriveled-up leaves and stubs? This flower is not coming back . . .* I was having this conversation with myself when my phone began to buzz. I answered the call and heard my friend's voice on the other end of the line.

As we exchanged benign greetings in that awkward way you do, when silence has distanced you for so long, I happened to be watering a mound of dead foliage. Twenty minutes into the restorative, forgiveness-drenched conversation that had been nineteen months coming—me forgiving him for the indiscretion, him forgiving me for the ensuing distance, us agreeing to move forward in humility and love—I was still resting on a rake in my front yard. Then I absentmindedly kicked over some mulch on that plant I just knew was dead. And that's when I saw it: the tiniest of tiny green shoots. It felt like a nod from God: *What you thought was dead isn't dead, Brady. I'm Master of all things new . . .*

Even as a young boy, I remember being fascinated with nature, with how trees could go to sleep and then, a season later, wake again. When I ended that call with my friend, I thought about winter, and spring.

God is a god of springtime, the Bible promises. *Behold*, he is doing new things.

The grandest story in all of history centers on God coming to earth in the form of a man, taking on the sin of all creation, and then voluntarily enduring the deepest, darkest death the world had ever known.

But then.

In a majestic display of grandeur and power, God raised his Son from the dead. "Then bursting forth in glorious day," the song says, "Up from the grave, He rose again!"[4] And in that moment of ultimate resurrection, we find the potential for all other resurrections to occur. God doesn't just bring trees back to life; he brings *us* back to life. Whatever has separated us—from him, from each other, from ourselves—can be brought together once more.

Let me give you a tip regarding relationships, courtesy of my beloved wife, Pam. Whenever I sink low because a friendship has waned or a professional tie has been cut or a family member quietly drifts, Pam reminds me that interpersonal connections are not static things; they're always bending and turning, shifting and changing, contouring to what's happening now. Therefore, we do better to hold them loosely, to let them chart the course they're compelled to chart. "Pay attention to the relationships that are in front of you," she says to me. "Put your best energies there. You don't have to push, or pry, or pursue anyone obsessively, when you trust the Lord to direct your steps."

You've probably heard of the anthropologist and psychologist Robin Dunbar, whose famous "Dunbar's number" detailed the highest number of stable relationships a person can sustain at any time. In his research, he found that a person can maintain only 150 casual friends, 50 close friends, 15 confidants, and 5 intimate friends.[5] When I factor in this information with Pam's counsel, I am reminded that I don't have a limitless capacity for relating with others and that naturally connections will be stronger at some points than at others, much like a cell phone's bars of signal strength. A "confidant" (five bars) who moves to a different state might become a "close friend" (three bars? four?) overnight. It's not that anything went wrong, per se; it's just that proximity can have that effect.

These days I have three adults living in my house with me: two teenagers and my wife. The emotional and spiritual investment this requires of me means that three-fifths of my "intimate friend" slots are full, leaving available spaces for only two more. This simple relational math has helped me to quit clinging to friendships as though my life depends on them, instead trusting that God will provide. It also helps me to forgive those who hurt me, knowing that those who leave may very well come back. In the same way that trees go to sleep and wake up, that staticky connection you and I have known can find clear air once again. *What I've seen you do in nature thousands of times,* we can say to God, *I trust you to do in my life.*

He'll do it—I truly believe that. Every stump can reveal a green shoot.

I have a homework assignment for you if you're up to it. It involves five minutes, three decisions, and one prayer. Before you put down this book and go about the day's business, find a quiet space where you can commune with God. In accordance with the Scriptures, first honor God for his holiness, his otherness, and his goodness. Express your awe over his magnificence and grace. You might pray the words of a psalm back to him, speaking to him in the first person, as you would to a friend.

Next, confess any sins that you're aware of, asking the Holy Spirit to prompt you toward this end.

Finally, tell God of your desire to become more gracious, to be known as a possessor of *truly remarkable grace*. Ask God to help you seize opportunities to be more accepting, to be kinder, to be more forgiving day by day. And then—and here's the "three decisions" part—determine to practice each of these traits.

Before God, I'm asking you to decide to be accepting, to be kind, and to be forgiving, so that as opportunities to display these characteristics present themselves, you've *already agreed* to say yes. When your right-wing colleague starts ranting to you at tomorrow's lunch about whatever the liberals have done now, having already decided to be accepting, you can say, "I get that you're upset . . . I can see that . . . I can hear how frustrated you are."

When your socialist teenage son talks about the evils of capitalist greed, having already decided to be kind, you can say, "Son, I don't always agree with your conclusions, but I always love knowing what you're thinking about . . . and I'll always admire your passion."

When your confidant betrays a privileged piece of information about your life next month, having already decided to forgive, you can say, "I love you. I forgive you. Let's work together to heal."

I could go on, but I think you catch my drift. Let's become the most gracious people the world has seen. *Remarkably* gracious, even, in a culture bent on tearing each other down.

6

A Different Kind of Pleasure Pursuit

We Can Reflect Remarkable Sexuality

Oh, Lord, give me chastity.
But do not give it yet.

SAINT AUGUSTINE

I came across an article from *Vanity Fair* not long ago that detailed the dating habits of today's singles, if you can call what is happening these days "dating," and felt a certain weight settle deep down in my gut. Reflecting on the uptick in his love life since the arrival of mobile dating apps such as Tinder, Happn, and Hinge, one twenty-something named Alex grinned: "You could talk to two or three girls at a bar and pick the best one," he said, "or you can swipe a couple hundred people a day . . . It's setting up two or three Tinder dates a week and, chances are, sleeping with all of them, so you could rack up 100 girls you've slept with in a year."

Another man interviewed, Dan, raved that apps like Tinder, which require only photographs instead of lengthy profiles and which allow users to quickly vet potential dates—swipe right to show interest, left to ditch—have made securing a hookup as easy as getting a pizza delivered. "It's like ordering [from the online food-delivery service] Seamless," he said. "But you're ordering a person."

The women the magazine surveyed were equally crass, talking with emotionally detached inflection about how challenging it is to find men on these sites who can actually "perform," attributing much of the problem to those dates' "skewed view of the reality of sex through porn."[1]

It would be nice to write off these examples as mere cultural anecdotes, surely exceptions to the current dating scene rule, but that's hardly the case. The Pew Research Center reports that one in three eighteen- to twenty-four-year-olds are users of online mobile dating apps, representing 300 percent growth in the past six years, and that attitudes toward the legitimacy of online mobile dating are only getting "progressively more positive."[2] The efficiency and expediency of it all—not having to *actually get to know someone* before cutting to the chase and having sex with him or her—is a self-perpetuating thing, according to many research study respondents. *When it's so easy, when it's so available to you,* the thinking goes, *it's so hard to contain yourself.*

This lack of containment, this lack of self-control, seems to be at the core of many sexual trends these days.

The *Vanity Fair* piece was one of a whole host of online articles, book excerpts, and research studies I've seen that detail today's sexual mores, each one more disturbing than the last. The findings that bombarded me I'll now bombard you with:

- Today, one in eight online searches and one in five mobile searches is for porn.[3]
- Porn sites account for a full one-third of the Internet's bandwidth.[4]
- Ninety-three percent of boys and 62 percent of girls are exposed to pornography before age eighteen, with more than half of those reporting first views prior to age *eight*.[5]
- One-third of all marriages today began as a hookup, which in almost every case meant both partners had been sexually active before meeting each other.[6]
- Nine in ten hookups involve drinking, and 35 percent of them involve heavy drinking.[7]
- Incidents of sexually transmitted disease—including syphilis, chlamydia, and gonorrhea—are on the rise, with half of the nearly 20 million new infections each year occurring in young people ages fifteen to twenty-four.[8]
- Globally, during the period from 2010 to 2014, there were 56 million abortions performed annually.[9]

If you think that as a society we objectify the human body to the point of our detaching it from the soul inside, then you are correct.

If you think that we grossly commercialize sex, and do so without remorse, then you are correct.

If you think that people both inside and outside the church consider "rules" against fornication (if anyone still even knows what that means) outdated and somewhat "quaint," then you are correct.

If you think that collectively we regard perversion as just "staying true to our desires," then you are correct.

If you think that we do not regard the weighty consequences of our sexual habits, behaviors, and preferences as consequential at all, then you are correct.

If you think that these and a whole host of similar trends are *true*, then you are correct.

If you think that these things are *new*, then you're not.

When the apostle Paul set foot in the city of Corinth, he found a level of sexual brokenness and deviance that just might put our current trends to shame. I referenced earlier the temple of Aphrodite, and while it indeed was home to truly abhorrent practices—women by the thousands who had no other options in life because they were exploited as temple prostitutes—the temple was simply a reflection of the Corinthian culture at large.

Further, even if a woman was able to find a man willing to marry her, her lot remained sorry in life. Women were regarded as property—and disposable property at that. They were good for having sex. They were good for raising kids. There were good, in Greek men's eyes, for little else.

So, in Corinth, Paul found rampant sexual perversion. He found rampant chauvinism. He found soul-squelching deviance. And he found these things *inside the church*.

It's often overlooked that, despite its name, the book of

1 Corinthians does not reflect the apostle Paul's first communication to the Corinthian church. In fact, Paul had spent lots of time with this group of believers six years prior, during his second of three missionary journeys throughout Europe, living with them, for instance, in AD 50, when he penned his first letter to believers in Thessalonica. During that time Paul surely trained the Corinthian church in the ways of Jesus, reminding them of the values of humility and mercy, of the priorities of righteousness and godliness, of the quest for the kingdom of heaven, of honesty, of kindness, of peace.

As it related to sex and sexuality, Paul surely recounted Jesus' expansion of the old covenant law. "You have heard the commandment that says, 'You must not commit adultery,'" Jesus taught. "But I say, anyone who even looks at a woman with lust has already committed adultery with her in his heart" (Matthew 5:27–28). This elaboration made it clear that sex is not merely a physical act but an emotional and spiritual one as well. The sexual acts engaged in with the body, in other words, have their beginnings inside the *heart*.

Sex *matters* to God, Paul wanted them to understand. Sex is a *gift* from God. Believers' sexual practices either *honor* God, or else they don't.

Paul had labored with this church at Corinth, determined to set them up for success. He had poured himself into them faithfully, discipling them for years on end. He had done his level best to impart to them the deepest spiritual wisdom he had found. And now this: Word comes to Paul that they are forsaking the lessons they'd learned. Believers who knew better were sleeping with prostitutes. Believers who knew better were practicing incest. Believers who knew better were pretending their bodies were their own. But perhaps worse than these actions were their attitudes: these believers who had chosen such sexually deviant behavior *were not troubled by these choices at all.*

In my twenty years of pastoral ministry, I have detected a significant shift in the way believers refer to what most of us who follow Jesus would consider errant behavior: behavior that stands in stark contrast to the "way of Christ." My oversimplification of that shift is this: there was a time when shameful behavior *actually produced shame in the one who'd exhibited it*. In the same way that Adam and Eve, aware that they had sinned against God, went in search of fig leaves to cover their naked loins, I distinctly recall an era when Christians who did decidedly unchristian things felt embarrassment, remorse, and regret.

This is what Paul found so frustrating, upon hearing of the Corinthians' sin. "I can hardly believe the report about the sexual immorality going on among you—something that even pagans don't do," he wrote to the church there. "I am told that a man in your church is living in sin with his stepmother. You are so proud of yourselves, but you should be mourning in sorrow and shame. And you should remove this man from your fellowship" (1 Corinthians 5:1–2).

The action? A man was "living in sin," having sexual relations with his own stepmother. The attitude *about* the action? The church was *proud* instead of *ashamed*.

A few verses later, regarding this flippant attitude toward sin, Paul writes, "Your boasting about this is terrible. Don't you realize that this sin is like a little yeast that spreads through the whole batch of dough? Get rid of the old 'yeast' by removing this wicked person from among you. Then you will be like a fresh batch of dough made without yeast, which is what you really are" (vv. 6–7).

Paul's counsel was swift and severe: *Part ways with the sinful man.*

Verse 5 said it this way: "Then you must throw this man out and hand him over to Satan so that his sinful nature will be destroyed and he himself will be saved on the day the Lord returns."

Pretty harsh, don't you think?

The teacher went on to explain to his wayward students that, because Christ, the Passover Lamb, had been sacrificed for them, "so let us celebrate the festival, not with the old bread of wickedness and evil, but with the new bread of sincerity and truth" (v. 8). In Jesus' day, Jews would prepare their household for Passover each spring by cleaning, by clearing away. They would literally get rid of the old things to make room for the new—among them new yeast, with which they would make the Passover meal. That little phrase of Paul's, "so let us," is key. "So let us" reflects both the power *to be able to do* what he is instructing these believers (and us) to do, and "so let us" reflects the compulsion *to actually do it*.

Now, before we move on, it's important to note that Paul's instruction regarding this man who was sleeping with his stepmother was harsh because the man was professing Christ while indulging incestuous sexual sin. In verses 9 through 13 he said as much: "When I wrote to you before, I told you not to associate with people who indulge in sexual sin. But I wasn't talking about unbelievers who indulge in sexual sin, or are greedy, or cheat people, or worship idols. You would have to leave this world to avoid people like that.

"I meant that you are not to associate with anyone who claims to be a believer yet indulges in sexual sin, or is greedy, or worships idols, or is abusive, or is a drunkard, or cheats people. Don't even eat with such people.

"It isn't my responsibility to judge outsiders, but it certainly is your responsibility to judge those inside the church who are sinning. God will judge those on the outside; but as the Scriptures say, 'You must remove the evil person from among you.' "

So this man was an earnest spiritual seeker, someone who had come to the church looking for help. Both then and now, the church is intended to be a hospital for the wounded, the rejected, the dejected, and the hurt. Our doors are to be swung wide open to the messiest of messy folks. But upon helping those folks encounter the risen Christ, there is to be a moment of reckoning when those people acknowledge their need for him. Upon professing that need and signaling a desire to grow in Christ, transformation is to have its way. The "old life is gone; a new life is begun!" 2 Corinthians 5:17 declares.

This man was trying to have it both ways. He had taken hold of this "new life in Christ" while still clinging to the sinfulness of his past. Instead of fighting for purity, he was flaunting his sin—an affront to his fellow believers and God alike. He was a card-carrying Christian, a key member of the

Corinthian church, who was celebrating what God despised. He hadn't asked for help because he didn't *need* any help—at least, not according to him. We might say of his actions that he was "following his heart"; what's so bad about that?

A few years ago I was sitting at breakfast with a young man I was trying to persuade toward the things of Christ, when I received a prompting from God. The young man was a self-proclaimed follower of Christ who was hip-deep in unrepentant sin. I had carved out large chunks of my schedule over a months-long period of time to try to help him see the folly of his ways, turn away from those ways, and go God's way instead. He would have none of it. That morning at breakfast, where for the dozenth time he was checking his phone instead of listening to what I had to say, the Lord all but audibly whispered to me, "Brady, he hasn't had enough of the world yet . . ."

> Our doors are to be swung wide open to the messiest of messy folks.

This young man still believed that the world had something special to offer to him, something better than what Christ could provide. Until he grew completely frustrated with the façade of the world, he would have no need for Jesus, for truth.

I sat there watching the young man as he stared at his phone. I resolved in my heart to love him, to care for him, and to be there for him when it all fell apart. I feared it *would* all fall apart, and when he finally grew sick and tired of being sick and tired, I would be there to help him come home. Until that point I knew that I had to turn him over to the desires of his flesh, because his flesh is all he cared about.

See, this is exactly what Paul exhorted the Corinthian church to do. He wasn't suggesting that those believers put some curse or hex on the man. He simply knew that sometimes we must run our own truth into the ground before we have ears to hear the truth of God.

It is my belief that pastors as a rule hate preaching on two topics. Any guesses as to what those are? They are the same topics that are known to derail marriages, fell corporate leaders, and strike fear in the hearts of parents worldwide: money and sex. Money and sex: Who wants to talk about that? Well, I do. And the apostle Paul did. Why? Because the stakes are too high not to. As it relates to our topic at hand, just as violence can kill the body, sex can kill the soul. But equally true is this: when we win the battle over sexual deviance, which centers on whose plan we will follow and whose glory we will seek, we win *purity* for the church. Purity, as you may recall, is what Christ expects from his Bride, the church. "He gave up his life for her [the church]," Ephesians 5:25–27 reminds us, "to make her holy and clean, washed by the cleansing of God's word. He did this to present her to himself as a glorious church without a spot or wrinkle or any other blemish."

Holy.

Clean.

Washed by the cleansing of God's word.

No wrinkles.

No blemishes.

No spots.

Now, we know why Paul told the Corinthians to part ways with the man who was celebrating his sin, agreed? He was slashing to shreds the Bride's bright-white wedding dress and splattering paint across her face. Just *egregious*, in Paul's view. It ought to be in our view too. We will never stand out as *remarkable* in this world apart from prizing the purity God says we must prize.

Believers are to preserve this purity Christ has given to us, to fight for it with all they've got. In other words, we have been given the power to exhibit self-control in our sexuality; we need only begin wielding that power. In the same way that a little leaven can spoil the whole batch, a little purity can be used for great good. It is this purity that will make us remarkable in a world that has elevated its own will far above God's.

It is this purity that will make us remarkable in a world that has elevated its own will far above God's.

In the sixth chapter of 1 Corinthians, Paul lays out a "purity plan," if you will, that we, too, would be wise to adopt. There he reimagines our sexual experience and reminds us of God's better way. Let me give you the text first and then extract the key lessons we find.

> *You say, "I am allowed to do anything"—but not everything is good for you. And even though "I am allowed to do anything," I must not become a slave to anything. You say, "Food was made for the stomach, and the stomach for food." (This is true, though someday God will do away with both of them.) But you can't say that our bodies were made for sexual immorality.*

> *They were made for the Lord, and the Lord cares about our bodies. And God will raise us from the dead by his power, just as he raised our Lord from the dead.*
>
> *Don't you realize that your bodies are actually parts of Christ? Should a man take his body, which is part of Christ, and join it to a prostitute? Never! And don't you realize that if a man joins himself to a prostitute, he becomes one body with her? For the Scriptures say, "The two are united into one." But the person who is joined to the Lord is one spirit with him.*
>
> *Run from sexual sin! No other sin so clearly affects the body as this one does. For sexual immorality is a sin against your own body. Don't you realize that your body is a temple of the Holy Spirit, who lives in you and was given to you by God? You do not belong to yourself, for God bought you with a high price. So you must honor God with your body [1 Corinthians 6:12–20].*

Whew: Paul doesn't exactly mince words. In case you are presently practicing sexual behaviors that wouldn't be considered "holy and pure," let me begin where the apostle Paul left off: "*Run from sexual sin!*"

TO PRIZE PURITY, REPENT

We looked in the last chapter at the story of the woman caught in adultery from John 8. You'll recall that after Jesus defused the situation and prompted the woman's accusers to drop their stones and depart, he engaged her with five simple words: "Go and sin no more."

Go and sin no more.

These words were an invitation—into power, into repentance, into grace. "Go and sin no more" implied that the woman possessed the power to follow through. She could go. She could sin no more. These were choices that she could make.

"Go and sin no more" implied that the woman could chart a new course. *You've been going in one direction,* Jesus essentially said. *Now turn. Go the other way.*

"Go and sin no more" implied that the woman could find the wholeness and healing she sought. *As you go, as you sin no more, you'll find life that is truly life.*

As I mentioned earlier, it is simply not enough for us to be convicted regarding sexual sin; *decisive action* is then required. Surveying the scene when Jesus stooped to write with his finger in the sand on which that adulterous woman stood, Pope John Paul II once said, "By his silence, Jesus invites all of us to self-reflection." Indeed, he does. Equally true, he compels us by his example to rise from that session of self-reflection and *act on what's been revealed.*

I found it interesting that in the *Vanity Fair* article I came across, despite interviewees admitting to being on apps such as Tinder as much as twenty hours a day,[10] when asked what they *think* of such apps and the practices that those apps seem to spur on, there was consensus in the room. It seems so obvious a question that it's hardly worth asking, isn't it? If a person is engaging in something pretty much every waking hour, isn't it a foregone conclusion that the person likes that thing? Isn't this the equivalent of asking a fish what it thinks of water or a pig what it thinks of mud? But when the interviewer posed the question—"What do you think of Tinder?"—the group agreed: "It sucks."[11]

Conviction is nothing apart from requisite action. We can know a thing is not helpful and yet still participate in that unhelpful thing.

On too many occasions these days, the other pastors and I are called in to counsel men and women alike who are wrestling with an addiction to porn. And on far too many occasions, while the one wrestling agrees that the addiction is causing undue harm to their life—it is captivating their thoughts, it is confusing their heart, it is squelching their spiritual growth—they simply cannot or will not quit.

I have been very open with my congregation regarding how I myself struggled with this particular sin when I was a young twenty-something. Which is how I know what I've said is true: *conviction is nothing apart from requisite action. We can know a thing is not helpful and yet still participate in that unhelpful thing.*

To any person struggling with sexual sin of any kind, Paul's words resound: Repent. Go a different way. *Run from sexual sin!*

We can stop.

And turn.

And go the other way.

TO PRIZE PURITY, **BE WATCHFUL**

Becky is a colleague of mine at New Life, and she tells a story from decades ago, when she was in her early twenties and newly married to David, and both were working at the same church. Becky noticed over a period of a few weeks that another church associate was making a habit of stopping by her office and that increasingly his comments were becoming more personal in nature. At first he would just say hi and ask how her day was going, but soon those remarks morphed into observations about her outfit, her new haircut, her smile. Becky grew uncomfortable; something just seemed off. She knew this man and considered him a friend, as was his wife, whom she'd socialized with. But an invisible line had somehow been crossed. She knew it. She wanted it to stop.

After another of this man's frequent drop-ins, Becky headed for her husband's office, closed the door behind her, and said, "David, something isn't right . . ." She explained what had been happening and then asked what she should do.

"Well," David said, "let's pray . . ."

David held Becky's hands, and together they prayed that light would overtake darkness, that Becky would be protected, that this other man would relent, and that righteousness would prevail. Becky exhaled relief and went back to her office. Which is when her desk phone rang.

On the other end of the line was a family friend from another state, a pastor named Tim who hadn't talked to Becky or

David in weeks. Tim's voice was urgent. "Becky," he said, "I'm just going to tell you the prompting I received from God. Becky, a trap has been set for you, and God is telling you to *run*."

Becky nodded her head and said to Tim, "Yep. I'm on it. You're right."

Fortunately, the man quit coming around. Believing the situation had resolved itself, Becky and David moved on.

Nine months later Becky received a call from the man's wife. Through tears, she told Becky that she believed her husband was cheating on her and that he and the other woman were together at that very moment. Becky and David left the church and drove to the woman's house, arriving just as her husband was getting home. As a result of a long, agonizing confrontation, the truth came tumbling out. For nine months the man *had* been having an affair, with another woman on the church staff. The wife's suspicions were proven correct.

The couple decided to fight for their marriage and work through the pain of the affair. That night, as they were leaving the couple's home, David nudged Becky and said, "Tell him."

Becky knew what David meant. Looking at the man, she said, "It's just that last year, about this same time, it seemed like you were coming on to me."

The man hung his head. "I was," he admitted. "I couldn't get you, but I got her."

The apostle Peter once wrote to believers: "Stay alert! Watch out for your great enemy, the devil. He prowls around like a roaring lion, looking for someone to devour. Stand firm against him, and be strong in your faith" (1 Peter 5:8–9).

Stay alert! Or, as one commentator put it, "Rouse yourself to watchfulness." Or, more to the point, "Wake up! Look up! Watch where you're planting your feet!"

Satan loves to plant land mines along our path to righteousness. This is why three chapters in a row inside the book of Proverbs harp on the idea of steering clear of such devious traps. Here's a sampling in case you're unfamiliar with the text:

> *The lips of an immoral woman are as sweet as honey, and her mouth is smoother than oil. But in the end she is as bitter as poison, as dangerous as a double-edged sword . . .*
>
> *Her [the immoral one's] feet go down to death; her steps lead straight to the grave. For she cares nothing about the path to life. She staggers down a crooked trail and doesn't realize it.*
>
> *So now, my sons, listen to me. Never stray from what I am about to say: Stay away from her! Don't go near the door of her house!*
>
> *You will say . . . "Oh, why didn't I listen to my teachers? Why didn't I pay attention to my instructors? I have come to the brink of ruin, and now I must face public disgrace."*
>
> *Drink water from your own well—share your love only with your wife. Why spill the water of your springs in the streets, having sex with just anyone? You should reserve it for yourselves. Never share it with strangers.*

Why be captivated, my son, by an immoral woman, or fondle the breasts of a promiscuous woman? For the Lord sees clearly what a man does, examining every path he takes.

An evil man is held captive by his own sins; they are ropes that catch and hold him. He will die for lack of self-control; he will be lost because of his great foolishness.

My son, obey your father's commands, and don't neglect your mother's instruction. Keep their words always in your heart . . . When you walk, their counsel will lead you. When you sleep, they will protect you . . . For their command is a lamp and their instruction is a light; their corrective discipline is the way to life.

Love wisdom like a sister; make insight a beloved member of your family. Let them protect you from an affair with an immoral woman, from listening to the flattery of a promiscuous woman.[12]

And then the writer of Proverbs offers this haunting closing scene: "While I was at the window of my house, looking through the curtain, I saw some naive young men, and one in particular who lacked common sense. He was crossing the street near the house of an immoral woman, strolling down the path by her house. It was twilight, in the evening, as deep darkness fell. The woman approached him, seductively dressed and sly of heart. She was the brash, rebellious type, never content to stay at home . . . She threw her arms around him and kissed him, and with a brazen look she said, 'I've just made my peace offerings and fulfilled my vows. You're the one I was looking for! I came out to find you, and here you are!

"'My bed is spread with beautiful blankets, with colored sheets of Egyptian linen. I've perfumed my bed with myrrh, aloes, and cinnamon. Come, let's drink our fill of love until morning. Let's enjoy each other's caresses, for my husband is not home. He's away on a long trip . . .'

"So she seduced him with her pretty speech and enticed him with her flattery. He followed her at once, like an ox going to the slaughter. He was like a stag caught in a trap, awaiting the arrow that would pierce its heart. He was like a bird flying into a snare, little knowing it would cost him his life" (Proverbs 7:6–23).

We see that man about to enter that woman's home, the married woman's home, and everything in us screams, *Doooooon't gooooo!* We know better. *He* knows better. And yet, too often, he goes anyway. Which is why we do well to stay watchful, to stay on guard.

"Don't you realize that if a man joins himself to a prostitute, he becomes one body with her?" the apostle Paul wrote in 1 Corinthians 6:16. "For the Scriptures say, 'The two are united into one.'" Sex acts are never merely physical; they are emotional and spiritual too. Engage your *heart* as you make sexual decisions. And also engage your *mind*.

TO PRIZE PURITY, **CHOOSE TO LOVE WELL**

Perhaps the weightiest theme in Paul's counsel to the Corinthians is for them to boldly choose to love well.

To understand why Paul would connect the ideas of sexual purity and Christlike love, we have to understand the heart of God. From the beginning, God has been a god of boundaries. During the creation of the world, Proverbs 8:29 confirms, God "set the limits of the seas, so they would not spread beyond their boundaries."

In the Garden of Eden, it was God who set off the Tree of the Knowledge of Good and Evil, telling Adam and Eve to eat from any tree they wished *except for that particular tree*.

In Exodus 20, God hands his people, the nation of Israel, a list of clear "boundaries," or commandments—ten, to be exact.

Throughout the book of Leviticus, God dispenses a whole series of boundaries regarding proper worship and right living.

Continuing on in the Old Testament, God put forth boundaries regarding keeping in step with him, boundaries regarding keeping civil peace, and boundaries regarding keeping one's own heart pure.

Shifting to the New Testament, we find boundaries that deal with a whole host of daily considerations: work, rest, service, achievement, money, leadership, friendship, hospitality, love, and, of course, sex.

In the Old Testament, which reflects God's covenant with the nation of Israel, these boundaries disempower even the most committed soul from living a life of supernatural strength. God knew that the Hebrew people could not uphold the hundreds of laws they were to live by, subsets of God's original ten, and so, the thinking went, in their inadequacy, they would turn toward the one truly adequate God.

But in the New Testament, which reflects God's covenant with individual hearts who are committed to him, these boundaries *empower a truly surrendered soul to live a life of supernatural strength.*

It's this New Testament reality that's ours. Meaning, whenever we're reading along in the New Testament and we find a clear boundary line that Jesus has drawn, we can rest assured that staying within that boundary will lead us to life that is truly life. We will be dispensers of *grace*. And that's how this fits in with the message of this book. Peace is grace, kindness is grace, acceptance is grace, purity is grace.

Peace is grace, kindness is grace, acceptance is grace, purity is grace.

When Jesus says that *as much as it depends on us, we must live at peace,* he is saying: "If you will live in peace, then you will find life that is truly life.

This is the grace of God.

When Jesus says to *honor other people above ourselves,* he is saying: If you will put your needs second and become an others-first kind of person, then you will find life that is truly life.

When Jesus says to *carry each other's burdens,* he is saying: If you will look beyond your own self-interest and help others to shoulder their loads when those loads are too weighty for them to bear, then you will find life that is truly life.

When Jesus says to *extend the same lavish forgiveness to those who hurt us that Christ himself has extended to us*, he is saying: When you refuse to hold on to bitterness, you are free to live life that is truly life.

I could go on, but I think you get the point. Now let me momentarily push "pause."

Harkening back to a scene we looked at in chapter 3, let me draw your attention to the day when Jesus was teaching people about the kingdom of God and religious experts showed up to try to trap him with a question. "Teacher," they asked, "which is the most important commandment in the law of Moses?" (Matthew 22:36).

Referring first to the Hebrew law noted in Deuteronomy 6:5, Matthew 22:37–40 explains: "[Jesus said], 'You must love the Lord your God with all your heart, all your soul, and all your mind.' This is the first and greatest commandment. A second is equally important: 'Love your neighbor as yourself.' The entire law and all the demands of the prophets are based on these two commandments."

So much is bound up in these words, but do you see what's peeking through? The greatest commandments Jesus stated both center on L-O-V-E, *love*.

When we're loving the people who bear God's image well, we are loving well God himself. When we're loving well the people whom Jesus died to save, we are loving Jesus himself. And how, exactly, do we love people well? *By honoring the boundaries that God has drawn*. We pray for them. We serve them. We extend kindness to them. We offer forgiveness to them. We treat them with humility. We treat them with compassion. We treat them with gentleness. We put their cares above ours.

You know what else we do?

We treat their bodies not as billboards but as sacred, holy space.

Once again, from Paul:

> *You can't say that our bodies were made for sexual immorality. They were made for the Lord, and the Lord cares about our bodies. And God will raise us from the dead by his power, just as he raised our Lord from the dead.*
>
> *Don't you realize that your bodies are actually parts of Christ? . . .*
>
> *For sexual immorality is a sin against your own body. Don't you realize that your body is a temple of the Holy Spirit, who lives in you and was given to you by God? You do not belong to yourself, for God bought you with a high price. So you must honor God with your body [1 Corinthians 6:13–15, 18–20].*

I can't tell you the number of times I've been approached, after preaching on the topic of sex, by men and women alike who say something along the lines of *What grown men and women do in their own bedrooms is their business, and their business, alone.*

I would be offended by their comments, except that the boundaries regarding sex—that it is reserved for marriage, and that it is to be between one man and one woman—were never my idea. This boundary came from Jesus, not me . . . The annoyance should be directed toward him.[13]

You know, in all compassion, this person is far from alone. Most people really like Jesus, until he starts messing with their sex lives. They like Jesus' justice, Jesus' concern for the poor, Jesus' love for innocents like widows and kids . . . but once he starts opining on what happens in our bedrooms? "No, thanks, Jesus . . . You can leave now."

Every rational person I know would agree that sexual abuse such as rape, incest, and abortion is always a devastating thing. Now, they might not be able to articulate exactly *why* these acts are so terrible, but they find themselves cringing all the same. The reason behind their discomfort is this: whenever we violate a human being, we violate someone who is divine. Genesis 1 confirms that God created every person, male and female alike. He created us in his image, the *imago Dei*, and there are spiritual implications to this. When we take the image of a woman, for instance, and use it for self-gratifying and superficial benefits, we attack the divine nature inherent in womankind. Satan loves this kind of thing. He abhors God's grand design.

Likewise, when we take the progression of intimacy espoused by Scripture—friendship leads to courtship, which leads to marriage, which leads to beautiful and satisfying sex—and reverse course, choosing to have sex right after learning the person's name and using that act to see if we want to be friends, we kick God's plan to the curb.

Further, when we take the singular act that allows two people to become one—sexual intercourse and all its trappings—and we cheapen it to a one-night stand, or an extramarital affair, or homosexual sex, we forcibly attack the divine nature inherent in the one we're with. We violate Jesus' wisdom on the issue, which is that sex is a gift from God, that like all worthwhile things sex is worth waiting for, that sex is to be enjoyed inside the covenant of marriage—one woman to one man. We may assume a posture of nonviolence in the world, but violent is exactly what we are.

Aw, come on, Brady . . . You're taking this all way too seriously . . .

I wonder if the woman whose Tinder hookup was already swiping on his app again—while she's still there—would think I'm taking things too seriously here.

The evidence says that she might. But I don't.

I wonder if the multiple women who, according to his own written confession, were unwittingly exposed to comedian Louis C.K.'s genitalia following various shows[14] would think I'm taking things too seriously here.

They may not agree that the solution is heterosexual marriage only, but would they not agree that perversion is a problem?

I wonder if the scores of men who confess to me their pornography addiction—an addiction that in their estimation will forever wreck their ability to have sex with their wives with a clear mind . . . I wonder if they would think I'm taking things too seriously here.

Seriousness is how Jesus seemed to treat this category of sin, anyway. "If your eye causes you to sin," he once told his followers, "gouge it out and throw it away. It's better to enter eternal life with only one eye than to have two eyes and be thrown into the fire of hell" (Matthew 18:9).

I wonder if the future husbands and wives of all the dating app hookups—men and women who will gladly and yet *pains-*

takingly need to navigate their life partner's trauma, regret, and perhaps sexually transmitted disease—I wonder if they would think I'm taking things too seriously here.

Ultimately the "rules" that Jesus put forth and Paul later proclaimed regarding our sexual practices centered on one reason and one reason alone: *We can't love people well when we step over those boundary lines.*

And when we cannot love people, we cannot love God. Which is a problem for us "lovers of God."

A few weeks ago a young man in our congregation proposed to his girlfriend of two years, and a huge celebration ensued. This man, Victor, and this woman, Preem, have literally grown up in our church. Nobody is more adventuresome than Victor, and nobody is more loving than Preem. Preem is sort of our "church daughter" in that *every* family claims her as theirs. (Her dad is a worship pastor on our staff and sees firsthand every Sunday, as Preem pinballs from one hug to the next, how absolutely this is true.)

Victor and Preem are barely twenty years old, and yet they would probably be considered old souls. Certainly, they'd be considered *old-school*. They never dated another person. Heck, they didn't even date each other, choosing to practice intentional "courtship" instead. They didn't hold hands for months after Victor requested (and received) permission from Preem's dad to pursue his girl. It was a big, big deal when Victor finally mustered the courage to peck Preem on the cheek.

Say what you will about antiquated values, about wanting "experience" before you commit, but to look at this young couple is to see a freedom anyone would want. It is to see a beautiful response to the call to "give honor to marriage" in Hebrews 13:4. Don't we all want to be part of a movement that honors God's boundaries instead of our own? Don't we all want to contribute to believers being *remarkable* once again? Don't we all long to honor others in the same way that we want to be honored ourselves?

Forget prudish behavior.

Forget puritanical norms.

Don't we deep down want to be *pure*?

I am convinced that God will help us reimagine our sexuality, if only we'll invite him in. I am convinced that he will fulfill the desires we once thought only sex could fulfill. I am convinced that the church can present herself as spotless to Jesus, having faithfully exhibited the grace of God. I am convinced that "remarkable" can describe us, even in this day of perversion and pain.

7

To Say Yes, to Stand Firm, to Shine

We Can Build Remarkable Marriages

The real act of marriage takes place in the heart, not in the ballroom or church or synagogue. It's a choice you make—not just on your wedding day, but over and over again—and that choice is reflected in the way you treat your husband or wife.

BARBARA DE ANGELIS

Last I checked, the divorce rate still hovers at around 50 percent, a rate that has no regard for self-proclaimed followers of Christ. Meaning: regardless of whether we're looking inside or outside the church, only one in two marriages will survive. This number has been relatively unchanged for the past forty years, so the stat itself should come as no surprise to you or me. What *might* surprise you is the reason all these marriages fail.

If I were to ask you about the most common causes for divorce, you might cite adultery or financial disagreements. You might cite addiction, or problems with sex, or workaholism, or porn. You might cite chronic breakdowns in communication. And you'd be right. These things *are* cited as culprits when couples choose to decouple these days.

What's not often discussed is the fact that these dynamics are merely symptoms of a deeper, more pervasive disease. The real culprit for that tragic 50 percent divorce rate is a little thing called *selfishness*—looking out for *me* despite God asking couples to live as *we*.

Reflecting on the consumer culture we've built and gladly indulge, Timothy Keller writes, "Both men and women today see marriage not as a way of creating character and community but as a way to reach personal life goals."[1] He calls this phenomenon the Me-Marriage, and its effects reach far and wide. To date, nobody seeking my input on how to repair their fractured marriage has opened with "Pastor Brady, our biggest issue is me. My selfishness. My ego. My inability to serve anyone else's needs but my own . . ." but that is, in fact, the case. Enjoying a "remarkable marriage" comes down to one straightforward task: removing *self* from the center of our lives.

"Satan has a clear-cut scheme for your marriage," I tell engaged women and men who come to me for premarital counseling these days, "and selfishness is it."

One day God had a dream. Seeing that the man, Adam, whom he created was all alone, he decided to give him a mate. Woman.

Taken from the side of man. Bone of his bone, flesh of his flesh, perfectly fitted to his physique. "Be fruitful," he told the first couple. "Multiply. Fill the earth and subdue it. Rule over all creation, over all creatures, over all things."

The two—one woman, one man—would leave their fathers and mothers and cleave not to their personal goals or their ministries or their mistresses or their jobs but to each other. They would walk together and talk together and see facets of God's character in each other that they'd never observed before. They would put each other's interests ahead of their own. They would become one in every sense of the word—emotional, physical, spiritual. They would be naked and unashamed, a picture of prosperity and joy. They would live together in harmony until death, mirroring the covenant between Jesus and his church. They would come together intentionally. They would work out their differences persistently. And they would stay the course till the end. They would show the watching world what true sacrifice looks like, true companionship, true partnership in ministry, true love.

This was God's dream from the beginning, intended to become reality for all time. God gave Adam and Eve everything they could possibly need for bringing glory to him and satisfaction to themselves—a job to do, the resources to do it, a beloved companion to do it with. He stood back, surveyed the scene, and declared it "very good"—the only part of creation, in fact, that was given the "very" nod.

And it *was* very good—that is, until humankind had its way. That dream of God's devolved into an outright nightmare as we twisted his straightforward plan.

We see evidence of the nightmare whenever a husband speaks harshly to his wife. We see evidence of the nightmare whenever a wife indulges a secret affair. We see evidence of the nightmare whenever a couple prizes addiction over each other. We see evidence of the nightmare whenever selfishness has its way. It's so *horrifying*, all these evidences, as nightmares always are. And yet these themes are hardly irreversible. *There is still hope for us.*

When the apostle Paul entered the city of Corinth, he saw trends that made his heart sink low. There was rampant sexual immorality. Husbands and wives were divorcing for no real cause. Husbands were refusing to meet their wife's sexual needs, and wives were refusing those of their husbands. Believers were marrying unbelievers, which was causing disharmony in their homes. People were becoming attached to the things of this world, marriage included, instead of to the mission God had asked them to pursue. These trends were pervasive. They were sinful. They were disheartening. And yet—according to Paul, anyway—they were not beyond repair.

Paul's noted his advice to the Corinthian believers in 1 Corinthians 7, a response, evidently, to at least one letter of inquiry they'd sent to him after he departed their presence to head to Ephesus. That response included such exhortations as:

- If you're a husband, have only one wife, and if you're a wife, have only one husband.

- Husbands, fulfill your wives' sexual needs, and, wives, fulfill your husbands' too.
- Spouses, willingly give authority to each other, recognizing that your bodies are not your own.
- Married couples, have plentiful sex! Don't deprive each other of sex.
- Husbands and wives, don't leave each other. Stay together over the long haul.
- Spouses, minister to each other. Be a *blessing* in each other's lives.
- Husbands and wives, don't be distracted by the things of this world. Let your marriages serve as powerful ministry partnerships that help you accomplish the work of God.

Paul's counsel to those who were single was to be content with that station in life. Being married makes life complicated; better to stay devoted, simply, to God. But in the same breath, Paul's counsel to those who had already wed, or who intended to marry someday, was to apply every ounce of effort and care to choosing to stay married well. The question, then, is how to get that done. How do married people stay married well?

My wife and I will soon celebrate thirty years of marriage, and for years now I have been intrigued with the topic of what keeps couples together—not "together" in the sense of "staying in this thing for the kids" but rather *together*—unified, harmonious, of one accord. What caused some couples to disintegrate—sometimes only months after saying "I do"—and others to keep flourishing for years and years? What were the happily wedded doing that the unhappily wed were not? How were they interpreting the rather vague instructions from the apostle Paul so that their daily habits reflected the kind of commitment, mutual submission, and wholehearted surrender about which he wrote?

In the world of psychology—which at its core is simply the attempt to understand why we think and do what we think and do—there are always helpful steps and stages to apprehending patterns in people's lives. AA has its Twelve Steps. Grief has its five stages. Abraham Maslow had his five-tier hierarchy of needs. I had to wonder: Was it possible to name the cues that signaled whether a marriage was blossoming or withering, whether things were looking up or looking down? Did certain patterns exist in marriages that grow and thrive, and also in those that don't?

Yes, it turns out, there were. And once I was focused on finding (and naming) them, they were ridiculously plain to see. A married person neither destroys nor preserves the marriage in a single day; there are additive steps either way. For those of us who are married, we're either building our marriage moment by moment or else we're slowly blowing it up. The best way to prevent the small steps to destruction is to replace them with small steps that strengthen and fortify.

If you long to experience the kind of marital relationship that God envisioned from the start, you can begin by first taking an honest look at what's captivating you right now in life.

What or who has captured your imagination? What are you fascinated by these days? What is enamoring you and exciting you? And how does your spouse fit into that scene?

If you're unsure how to answer these questions, let me give you a shortcut. The next time your spouse enters the room, pay attention to how you react. Do your eyes follow him across the room? Do you get up from where you're sitting so she doesn't have to come to you? Do you greet each other with a hug and a kiss? (Is there a little peck at least?) Or do you barely look up from what you're doing, mumble a "Hey," and wonder why you couldn't have married someone who doesn't breathe so loud.

Now, if your spouse only made a quick trip to the restroom, the fanfare I describe might be a bit much. But when you've been separated for a block of several hours or an entire workday, wouldn't a little *intention* serve you both well? Assess whether you're interested in your husband. Assess whether you're fascinated by your wife. Assess whether your spouse excites you any longer. Assess where you're pointing your attention these days.

Before blaming your spouse for any distance you feel between the two of you, talk about this distance with God.

Next, once you've made your assessment, bring those honest findings to God. Before blaming your spouse for any distance you feel between the two of you, talk about this distance with God. Before blaming your spouse for any distance you feel with God, work on bridging that gap yourself. The best marriages I know are made up of two people who are diligent about getting their deepest needs met by their heavenly Father so that they don't come to their spouse insecure, needy, and filled with doubt. They work out those issues in quiet times of solo reflection and prayer, thus bringing fulfilled hearts and lives to their spouse. Renowned physician and marriage and family therapist Ed Wheat said, "Some people talk of marriage as ideally a fifty-fifty proposition. The problem with this idea is that each person is always waiting for the other to do something first. With a one hundred–one hundred partnership, either partner acting with a 100 percent giving attitude will contribute to the total marriage, so that there will be a reciprocating love from the other partner."[2]

So: Look to God for the contentment, fulfillment, and peace that God, alone, can provide. And also: Don't ask your spouse to be him. When we ask our spouse to be God, it sets us up for disappointment, because that person simply can't provide the healing and wholeness that God alone can give.

Regardless of where you've been, what you've done, or whom you've done it with, you simply must come around to believing that healing is yours to be had. Paul reminded the church of Corinth of this very truth: "He will keep you strong to the end," he wrote in 1 Corinthians 1:8, "so that you will be free from all blame on the day when our Lord Jesus Christ returns."

God can strengthen you.

God can strengthen your spouse.

God can strengthen your marriage.

God can strengthen your bond.

The weakening you've known can be reversed. God longs to keep you strong till the end. Thoughts can change. Attitudes can change. Brains can change. Habits can change. Cravings can change. Patterns can change. *Everything can be changed.*

Communication styles can improve. Sexual brokenness can be made whole. Financial mismanagement can be redeemed. Sorrows can be worked through. I'm telling you, everything can change in an instant when God is given room to run. Can I give you just four (of multiple thousands) ways to give God the running room he desires? These four hold great transformation potential; these four might just save your life . . .

PRAYER

Years ago, more than a decade into my ministry, one couple entered my office at the church yelling so loudly at each other that I ushered them in and closed the door quickly, hoping the staff in the office near me hadn't heard the vulgar things they'd said. These two *hated* each other; the vitriol was evident to see. I'm pretty sure the only reason they'd scheduled an appointment with me, their pastor, was to get permission to call it quits. They both loved God, they said. They both loved our church. They both loved their kids. And yet their love for each other was long gone.

I didn't ask them what had caused this latest fight, but based on the few phrases I heard lobbed across the room it evidently had to do with "all your other women" and "your *constant* need for control" and "Well, I wouldn't need to control things if you would just do what you *&#%$* *say you're gonna do*!"

I thought I might have to physically separate these two. Who talks to each other like that?

I sat the husband and the wife down and said, "Listen, I would love to help you here, but I'm not sure there's anything I can do. You're clearly beyond reasonable help. You've already decided to divorce. You don't even realize how obnoxious you're being. I think I'd be wasting my time . . ." They both looked at me with incredulity. "What, you don't recognize that you're kind of at each other's throats?" I asked.

They looked at each other and then back at me. After a moment, the wife said quietly, "We never thought we were the divorcing type . . ."

I took a deep breath. Speaking slowly and clearly, I said, "I don't know all that you've been through, all that has brought you to this terrible place, but I do know that if anything positive is going to happen in your marriage, it is going to be a supernatural act."

I told the couple that I had a single task for them that week. "I want to meet with you again in seven days," I said, "and between now and then the only thing I want you to do differently than you're doing now is to pray for each other, in each other's presence, out loud, every day. Seven times between now and our next meeting, I want you to pray a *sincere prayer of blessing* over your spouse. No praying heaps of ashes on their head. No praying for the wrath of God to fall. Blessings—only blessings . . . *blessings* must make up your prayers. If you hit seven times, then we can talk again. If you fail to do this *even once*, then our meeting next week is off."

As they left my office and walked down the hall, the wife a few steps ahead of the husband, who was scowling as he tried to keep up, I thought, *There is no way they're coming back next week. There is no way they'll do what I've asked.*

To my shock, the couple came back. "You actually did the prayer thing?" I asked, to which the husband said, "Man, that was hard." He and his wife sat down across from each other, and I asked them to recount what they had prayed. From the sound of it, they had actually followed through on my request, even if mostly through tightly clenched teeth. I gave them the same task for the next seven days: prayers of blessing,in each other's presence, aloud, and surprisingly, they did it again.

For several weeks things went on this way, and each time I saw this couple's name on my calendar, I shook my head in disbelief. Not only were they continuing to pray for each other, but they were now sitting together in my office, *holding hands*. By asking God's blessing over their spouse's life, each had begun to catch God's vision for the other. Instead of staring at all the wrongs that had been done, they gazed upon what was possible. Did God really see potential in her? Did God actually believe he could be faithful again? Was God truly committed to transforming them? Would he indeed give them bright days ahead?

Once the full truth emerged regarding all that they had done to each other, the myriad ways *both* had broken their vows, I realized that this couple had a biblical justification for divorce. And yet, by the time that was on the table, divorce isn't what they desired. Like a good patient who takes the necessary medicine until the bottle is totally empty, this couple kept praying, kept showing up, kept shooting straight, kept working, until they were committed to each other once more.

I know it may not seem possible today, depending on where you are with your spouse, but to invite God into our painful places is to let healing begin to seep in. If you're ready to quit focusing on the wrongs that have been done and start focusing on what God can make right, then begin praying blessings over your spouse—in his or her presence if possible, and aloud. Pray for his past wounds to be healed. Pray for her future concerns to be put at ease. Pray for his courage to live by his convictions. Pray for her to know that she is loved.

I know it may not seem possible today, depending on where you are with your spouse, but to invite God into our painful places is to let healing begin to seep in.

Pray for wisdom in managing money.

Pray for strength in your work.

Pray for forgiveness to overshadow hurtfulness.

Pray for gratitude to flood your minds.

Trust God with the future of your union and see if he doesn't bless you richly as a result.

PRAISE

In the world of community development, the wisest leaders understand that to enter any environment and start tossing around solutions before thoroughly understanding the problems is to set everyone up for failure and pain. Far better to step back, be quiet, and observe what's already working right. "Appreciative inquiry," this approach is called, and it works in marriages too.

To be married is to be provided with endless reasons to be annoyed. He never picks up his dirty clothes. She sighs with exasperation every time she's told no. He is always late getting home from work. She rolls her eyes at the stories he tells at dinner parties. He micromanages her expenditures. She talks too loudly. He chews with his mouth open. She obsesses over her appearance. He won't open up emotionally. She patronizes. He ridicules. She snores. "I love being married," comedian Rita Rudner once said. "It's so great to find that one special person you want to annoy for the rest of your life."[3]

Truly, *all* spouses are annoying from time to time. And while we can poke fun at the plentiful reasons for this and chuckle our way down the list, little annoyances can add up to big problems if we're not diligent in noting the pleasurable things too.

Along the lines of practicing appreciative inquiry, whenever you're tempted to be annoyed with your spouse, try *praising* your partner instead. Catch your husband or wife doing something good and express gratitude for that one thing.

"You stopped what you were doing and looked at me just then when you knew I had something to say," you might offer. "Thanks . . . That felt really good."

"I noticed that you refilled the fridge with that sparkling water we plow through. That was a really considerate thing to do . . ."

> Whenever you're tempted to be annoyed with your spouse, try *praising* your partner instead. Catch your husband or wife doing something good and express gratitude for that one thing.

"Keeping this place running as smoothly as you do must occupy so much of your energy and time. I see your hard work and I'm thankful for it. You're a gift to the kids and me . . ."

"I know that things have been stressful at work this week, and yet you still made our date night happen. That was a really kind thing to do."

"I couldn't help but overhear you while you were talking on the phone just then. You're a great listener and a great friend."

What you choose to praise isn't nearly as important as caring enough to praise it. Quick note: If you say one such "praise phrase" and your spouse eyes you suspiciously and responds with "What gives?" you'll know it's been a while since you offered up praise. You might consider upping your game.

And once you do, here is what I promise you: the practice will change your life. Speak out what you see is working right and build on things from there. In this way you will say yes to progress, yes to growth, yes to transformation and newness and faith. There are laudable things happening in your marriage today. Will you have eyes to see them and a heart to receive them? Will you put words of praise to what's working well?

I love the apostle Paul's advice to men and women who find themselves married to someone who isn't a believer in Christ, not so much because of his actual counsel, but because of the assumption his counsel makes. In 1 Corinthians 7:12–16 he wrote:

> *If a fellow believer has a wife who is not a believer and she is willing to continue living with him, he must not leave her. And if a believing woman has a husband who is not a believer and he is willing to continue living with her, she must not leave him. For the believing wife brings holiness to her marriage, and the believing husband brings holiness to his marriage. Otherwise, your children would not be holy, but now they are holy. (But if the husband or wife who isn't a believer insists on leaving, let them go. In such cases the believing husband or wife is no longer bound to the other, for God has called you to live in peace.)*
>
> *Don't you wives realize that your husbands might be saved because of you? And don't you husbands realize that your wives might be saved because of you?*

Specifically, these words are meant to provide instruction to a man or woman who lives with an unbelieving spouse, but do you see the Paul's motivation here, the underlying assumption he boldly makes? It's there in the last two lines of the text. Take another look.

"Don't you wives realize that your husbands might be saved because of you?" he asserts. "And don't you husbands realize that your wives might be saved because of you?" And how will such "salvation" show up? It will show up as the unbeliever is *persuaded by the believer's holiness*, according to this same passage. "The believing wife brings holiness to her marriage," we read, "and the believing husband brings holiness to his marriage."

The sentiment is so obvious that we barely give it a second glance. *Well, of course a believer brings holiness to the marriage,* we think. *Believers are* holy, *right?* Not so fast. Pretend for a moment that you were married to an unbelieving spouse. (You very well may be in such a situation, which means you won't have to pretend at all.) Would your unbelieving spouse say that your kindness is *so remarkable* that it compels him to consider Christ?

Would your unbelieving spouse say that your gentleness is *so remarkable* that it compels her to consider Christ?

What about your patience? Your goodness? Your self-control? Your peace?

Is your tendency to use your words for the purpose of praise and encouragement *so remarkable* that you could say, along with Paul, *Watching world, unbelieving spouse included, imitate me as I imitate Christ*?

Well? Is it?

I've given you a simple starting point with the *Praise each other* exercise, but in fact you can start anywhere. Pick an attribute of Jesus you see manifested in the New Testament and practice that attribute with your spouse. Be the most loving person he knows. Be the most joyful person she knows. Be the most considerate person he encounters to all day. Be the most grateful one she can find. For the moment, set aside all grievances and allow God to do his good work. And then, when the time is right, when your spirit is right, when the tone of your home is one of peace, God by his Spirit will address the issues that have been holding you back. He will help you find your way.

INTIMACY

At last, the moment you've been waiting for, when a pastor tells you to have more sex.

Couples often wonder aloud during counseling sessions why their marriages have fallen flat, paying no mind to the fact that they haven't had intimate time together in weeks or even months. My counsel isn't exactly rocket science: Go on a date! Pursue each other! Enjoy sex! "The husband should fulfill his wife's sexual needs," Paul encouraged in 1 Corinthians 7:3, "and the wife should fulfill her husband's needs." Come together. Love each other. Give yourselves both this gift.

I know that there are plenty of situations that simply having sex cannot fix, but let me also be quick to say that there are plenty that it can. Yes, you may have some work to do in this area before sex is considered pleasurable or fun. But my strong encouragement, regardless of your situation, is to read the books you need to read, schedule the therapy appointments you need to schedule, and engage fully in the conversations with your spouse that simply must be had so that you can keep intimacy alive in your home.

God stands ready to help you in your process here, as weird as that may seem. *Talk to God? About sex? Is that even legal?* you may ask. Yes, yes, yes to all three. He will listen. He will guide you. He will heal. "Imagine if naked were normal and we weren't freaked out that God made us sexual creatures on purpose . . . Imagine if we saw our sexuality as normal, but sacred, and the act of sex as something godlike and holy and fun and playful . . ." my brilliant friend Nancy Houston wrote in her book *Love & Sex: A Christian Guide to Healthy Intimacy*. "If our sexuality and our spirituality were integrated, we might have frequent conversations with God such as: 'God, would you teach me how to make love to my husband [or wife]'?"[4]

I like her vision here. The God who knit us together intentionally cares that we experience marriage intimately. He designed it. He instituted it. He ordained it. And he called it (very) good. So: Come before him with your pretenses set aside. Express your heart to him, and your earnest desires. Ask him to heal whatever needs healing and release you from every last pain. Trust him to lead you into a future filled with the mystery and beauty of married-life sex.

FRIENDSHIP

Okay, last one: Give God room to work by finding an accountability partner other than your spouse. Tell that person about the struggles you're having at home. Covet that person's earnest prayers on your behalf. Keep short accounts with this person so that conversations can be brief if need be. Choose to *tell the truth* every time you converse, lest all this diligence be in vain. Now, to the question of who you should select.

When looking for an accountability partner, keep three simple guidelines in mind. The person you choose ought to be more spiritually mature than you are. This person ought to be living in close proximity to you, since face-to-face meetings are best. And this person ought to be someone who can actually help you with the types of issues you face.

One final word on this topic, and then we'll move ahead: in 1 Corinthians 15:55–57, Paul reminds believers at Corinth that one day death's sting will be swallowed up whole. In other places, we read that *sin* is that sting of death, which means that the selfishness, rebellion, and pride we indulge in will one day meet their demise. Wisdom, then, would advise us to hitch our wagons to far different stars. Why attach to a fading endeavor? Why give ourselves over to that which will fail?

The purpose of seeking out strong accountability is to remind you of your longed-for success. Tell a trusted friend that you are *absolutely committed* to going wisdom's way in your life. And then ask for that person's help in keeping that vow.

There are real benefits to building a remarkable marriage, a marriage that stands firm and shines. First, we get to reap the blessings of perseverance, which are reserved for those who persevere. Second, we get to live *truly united* to our spouses, which is a picture of Christ and his church. Third, we get to see a fuller picture of who God is through the "otherness" of our spouse. And fourth, we get to model *something worth pursuing,* both to our children and to unmarried friends.

Most every marriage starts out remarkable, wouldn't you agree? The jittery groom standing at the altar, the bedazzled bride making her way down the aisle, the guests in abundance cheering on this new couple, all the hopes and dreams and potential two hearts can hold. My contention is that whatever has waned since that magical date can be reclaimed—that, and more. You and your spouse can share space comfortably, you can experience unabashed prosperity in the presence of God, you can live life fulfilled as man and wife, and you can *remarkably* stay the course.

8

All of You, All the Time

We Can Be Remarkable Worshippers of God

Worship is a way of seeing the world in the light of God.

ABRAHAM JOSHUA HESCHEL

The question isn't whether you're craving something today; the question is *what that thing is*. This craving I'm referring to is encouraging you to think, say, and do certain things and *not* to think, say, and do others. It is pushing you to find fulfillment—whatever that "filling" requires. This central craving of yours—for stimulation or for companionship, for good news or for relief, for affirmation or pleasure or peace—it's dictating more in your life than you may know. It is compelling you toward people and situations; it is cautioning you to steer clear of others. It is occupying your thoughts, it is scripting your words, it is manipulating your movements, it is influencing how you behave.

So, back to the driving question: *What is it that you crave?*

I know people who crave perfection. They work tirelessly

to improve every aspect of life, keeping endless to-do lists in hopes that if they can just organize things a little more, keep tracks of things a little better, whip just a little more of life into blissful submission, *then* they will be satisfied.

I have friends who crave achievement. They're constantly gunning for "the next big thing," whether that's a contract they're trying to land, a deal they're trying to seal, a property they're trying to sell, a piece of legislation they're trying to push through, a ministry program they're trying to launch, or a group of people they're trying to serve.

I've met people who are such perpetual learners that the thing they crave more than anything else is more knowledge, more insight, more facts. Really, they can't get enough. On whatever subjects have captivated them, they want to know all there is to know.

Although I'm not much for hanging out at a gym, I know people whose cravings center on a faster mile, a cleaner diet, a stronger physique.

There are those who crave *harmony* more than anything, thinking, *Can't we all just get along?*

There are some who crave money.

There are some who crave power.

There are some who crave physical pleasure.

There are *millions* in this country alone who crave alcohol or drugs.

I wonder: What is it for you? What is it that *you* crave?

I have a theory that the most important thing about you and me is how we answer that singular question. More important than our personality type, our pedigree, our profession, where we've been, who we know, or what we can do, is our answer to the question: "What do you crave?"

When you know your central, defining craving, you understand both your motivation and your direction in life. Which is why, when the apostle Paul came to the believers gathered in Corinth, he worked to compel them to crave only Christ.

In the letter Paul wrote to the Corinthian church after he'd spent eighteen months living in close relationship to them, he reminded them of how dangerous it is to claim Christ while still preferring sin. He wrote:

> *I don't want you to forget, dear brothers and sisters, about our ancestors in the wilderness long ago. All of them were guided by a cloud that moved ahead of them, and all of them walked through the sea on dry ground. In the cloud and in the sea, all of them were baptized as followers of Moses. All of them ate the same spiritual food, and all of them drank the same spiritual water. For they drank from the spiritual rock that traveled with them, and that rock was Christ. Yet God was not pleased with most of them, and their bodies were scattered in the wilderness.*
>
> *These things happened as a warning to us, so that we would not crave evil things as they did, or worship idols as some of them did. As the Scriptures say, "The people celebrated with feasting and drinking, and they indulged in pagan revelry." And we must not engage in sexual immorality as some of them did, causing 23,000 of them to die in one day.*
>
> *Nor should we put Christ to the test, as some of them did and then died from snakebites. And don't grumble as some of them did, and then were destroyed by the angel of death. These*

> *things happened to them as examples for us. They were written down to warn us who live at the end of the age.*
>
> *If you think you are standing strong, be careful not to fall. The temptations in your life are no different from what others experience. And God is faithful. He will not allow the temptation to be more than you can stand. When you are tempted, he will show you a way out so that you can endure.*
>
> *So, my dear friends, flee from the worship of idols. You are reasonable people. Decide for yourselves if what I am saying is true [1 Corinthians 10:1–15].*

Wake up, Paul essentially said to them. *Stop craving evil things! You can't desire independence from Christ and simultaneously glorify God. The two objectives cannot coexist. One will always win out.*

Such "independence" for the Corinthians looked like infighting and immorality, like haughtiness, immaturity, and pride. Which begs the question: What does "independence from Christ" look like in *your* life today? What does it look like in mine? We cringe when Paul calls these things "evil," but evil is exactly what distance from God is.

A word picture that has been vital to my understanding of how to crave Christ—and no one or nothing else—comes from the opening lines of Psalm 42, which feature a deer, a stream, and God. "As the deer longs for streams of water," verses 1 and 2 read, "so I long for you, O God. I thirst for God, the living God."

If you ever went to church camp as a kid, it's quite possible you were taught a slow-ballad version of this passage that featured the deer not "longing" but "panting"—as in, "As the deer panteth for the water, so my soul longeth after Thee . . ." The original Hebrew word, *arag* (pronounced *aw-rag*) means to long for, to deeply desire, to intentionally seek. The reason I bring this up is that the picture the psalmist put forth for us is not about a hot, parched animal willing to lap up the first stagnant puddle it finds, but about an earnestly seeking creature intent on *wisely sating its thirst*. The deer will settle for nothing less than clear, flowing streams of life-giving water, and the psalmist says, *That's me too.*

Living in Colorado, it's not a stretch for me to imagine a literal deer as it encounters a literal flowing stream. With our rough, craggy topography, there are plenty of undulations in the rocky hillsides where small pools of water turn murky, muddy, and gray. Sure, the moisture might feel good on the deer's tongue, but the water hardly will satisfy. It's hot water. It's bug-infested water. It's potentially diseased water. Plus it's smelly and grainy and thick. *Yuck*. Why settle for that unsatisfying puddle when a rushing stream is there, within reach?

My wife will tell you that in the almost thirty years that we've been married, even as I boast about being a relative health nut who is super-careful about what I eat, I've experienced a few seasons when I'd eat so many meals from fast-food restaurants that if my power window had gotten stuck, I'd have starved. Which brings me to the motivation for all cravings that don't honor God: *convenience*. We crave stimulation, so we head to Starbucks. We crave companionship, so we scroll social feeds. We crave entertainment, so we click on Netflix. We crave sustenance, so we drive through the drive-through. Notice a theme among our preferred solutions? They're *convenient*, every one of them.

Why stretch and strain for the stream of living water when the mud and the muck are *right here*?

There are plentiful examples of our convenience-seeking behavior, but perhaps the two more pernicious manifestations of this foolishness are our worship of self and our worship of stuff. We want to matter, and we want to look good doing it. We'll do almost anything to get there fast.

We're all tempted toward worship of self.

And then there's the matter of *stuff*. Our houses, our condos, our clothing, our cars, our vacations, our sports gear, our food. Jesus said not to worry about what we eat or what we wear, but where would Instagram be without posts on these things? The greatest cause of disease in the developed world today is not cancer or heart failure or diabetes or stroke but the six-letter culprit known as stress. *Stress!* And what are we stressing about?

What we're wearing.

Where we're going.

What we're eating.

How we're looking.

Where we're working.

What we're driving.

And where we live.

We worry about getting the job, and then we worry that it's not the perfect fit. We worry about finding a life partner, and then we worry because marriage isn't as easy as we dreamed it would be. We worry about being able to have children, and then we worry that our kids aren't turning out right. There are so many things to worry about that fretfulness becomes a close friend. This fixing our eyes on our stuff and not God? *Evil cravings*, to use Paul's words. We make an idol of the illusion of control in our lives and then are shocked when reality thumbs its nose at us.

The lunacy of this pattern reminds me of the prophet Isaiah's Old Testament riff on idolatry, delivered to God's chosen ones. "How foolish are those who manufacture idols," he wrote (Isaiah 44:9). The blacksmith stands at his forge to make a sharp tool, pounding and shaping it with all his might.

> *"His work makes him hungry and weak. It makes him thirsty and faint. Then the wood-carver measures a block of wood and draws a pattern on it. He works with chisel and plane and carves it into a human figure. He gives it human beauty and puts it in a little shrine. He cuts down cedars; he selects the cypress and the oak; he plants the pine in the forest to be nourished by the rain. Then he uses part of the wood to make a fire. With it he warms himself and bakes his bread. Then—yes, it's true—he takes the rest of it and makes himself a god to worship! He makes an idol and bows down in front of it! He burns part of the tree to roast his meat and to keep himself warm. He says, 'Ah, that fire feels good.' Then he takes what's left and makes his god: a carved idol! He falls down in front of it, worshiping and praying to it. 'Rescue me!' he says. 'You are my god!'*
>
> *"Such stupidity and ignorance! Their eyes are closed, and they cannot see. Their minds are shut, and they cannot think.*

> *The person who made the idol never stops to reflect, 'Why, it's just a block of wood! I burned half of it for heat and used it to bake my bread and roast my meat. How can the rest of it be a god? Should I bow down to worship a piece of wood?'*
>
> *"The poor, deluded fool feeds on ashes. He trusts something that can't help him at all. Yet he cannot bring himself to ask, 'Is this idol that I'm holding in my hand a lie?'" [Isaiah 44:12–20]*

Two quick observations. First: We shake our heads at these "poor, deluded fools," and yet don't you and I both relate? Can *we* bring ourselves to ask the question, *Is this idol I'm holding a lie?*

The brand-new vehicle we financed last month, despite being up to our eyeballs in debt: *Is this idol I'm holding a lie?*

The insistence that we deserve better than the way our spouse has been treating us lately: *Is this idol I'm holding a lie?*

The puffed-out chest of entitlement: *Is this idol I'm holding a lie?*

The ridiculous tendency to make more commitments than the hours in a day can hold: *Is this idol I'm holding a lie?*

The third glass of wine, night after night: *Is this idol I'm holding a lie?*

The ceaseless hours spent Instagram scrolling: *Is this idol I'm holding a lie?*

The rampant posturing and self-promotion: *Is this idol I'm holding a lie?*

All the ways that I seek to meet my needs on my own: *Are these idols I'm holding a lie?*

My second observation is this: all of Israel's harried and

hurried gyrations don't seem very restful to me. In the passage above, you'll find some *serious* scurrying going on. The idolater *pounds* and *shapes* with all his might till he stands there "hungry and weak," the text says. Faint and thirsty too. He *measures* and *draws*, *works* with chisel and plane, *carving*, *cutting*, and *selecting*. He then *plants* and *warms* and *bakes* and *takes* the rest to bow down to. He *burns* and *roasts* and *keeps* himself warm and then *carves* to make his god. He *falls* down and *prays* and *worships* it . . . "Rescue me! You are my god!"

Can we bring ourselves to ask the question, *Is this idol I'm holding a lie?*

So much action, and for what possible end? To be considered a *fool*.

Now, contrast that frenetic activity with the scene from Psalm 42. There is a deer—a silent, sure-footed deer. I picture that deer standing at the edge of a mud puddle, spotting a crystalline stream just ahead . . . *longing* for streams of water, the text says. In my imagination, her feet are planted, her posture is straight, as she takes in her choices here. Nothing but the sound of flowing water and wheels turning—*I've got to get to that stream!*

Purposefully and patiently, stretching past muck and mud, she strains for that clear, crisp flow.

"Come to me, all of you who are weary and carry heavy burdens," Jesus said, "and I will give you *rest*" (Matthew 11:28; emphasis mine).

She stretches. She tastes. She swallows, exhales. Her thirst is at last fully quenched.

To have our thirst fully quenched by God is to be in his presence. To step into God's presence is to enter creativity, restoration, love. It is to know soul-level satisfaction. It is to be awestruck. It is to *thrive*. To worship God is to encounter God, and to encounter God is to be wowed. In his book *The Practice of Godliness*, author Jerry Bridges writes, "We understand the thought of serving God, of being busy in His work. We may even have a 'quiet time' when we read the Bible and pray. But the idea of longing for God Himself, of wanting to deeply enjoy His fellowship and His presence, may seem a bit too mystical, almost bordering on fanaticism. We prefer our Christianity to be more practical."[1]

We prefer this more "practical" version of Christianity—that is, until we *truly encounter God*. I stand by what I wrote before: to taste the pure, unadulterated worship of Christ is to have your appetite whetted for more. How, then, do we stretch to reach that taste? What is required of us? Simply this: saying *yes* to one thing and saying *no* to all else.

I think of Jesus' reference early in his ministry to the "narrow gate" we must enter if we hope to follow him. During his summation of his moral teaching, delivered before his disciples in the Sermon on the Mount, Jesus declared: "You can enter God's Kingdom only through the narrow gate. The highway to hell is broad, and its gate is wide for the many who choose that way.

But the gateway to life is very narrow and the road is difficult, and only a few ever find it" (Matthew 7:13–14). Here, too, he speaks of *intention*. In the first century, where gates of all sizes and shapes dotted the perimeter of major cities, Jesus' audience would have understood the implications of the "narrow gate." Vast caravans couldn't fit through the narrow gate. Herds of livestock couldn't fit through the narrow gate. Mountains of earthly possessions couldn't fit through the narrow gate. Just you and only you, one person walking alone, could fit through that slim space. The trappings would have to stay put.

In our day and age, the challenge is great. "You mean I can't bring in all my stuff?" we ask Jesus, who waits on the other side of that narrow gate. He responds by quietly shaking his head. To say yes to taking the hand of Christ in worship is to loosen our grip on all else. This is the no I was referring to: *no* to all that we long to hold on to as we claim to be worshipping God.

Our need for control can't fit through the gate.

Our popularity can't fit through the gate.

Our entitlement can't fit through the gate.

Our earning potential can't fit through the gate.

Our past accomplishments can't fit through the gate.

Our unwillingness to forgive can't fit through the gate.

Our impatience and judgmental spirit can't fit through the gate;

Our wild distractibility can't fit through the gate;

And finally: our worries and fears and stressors and grief can't fit through the gate.

What then, do we do with all these things that can't fit

through the gate? Leave them! They will have to stay put where they are.

Like many churches, at New Life we spend the first twenty or twenty-five minutes of every gathering singing songs to God in a time of praise and worship. Several weeks ago I couldn't help but note that three of the families standing right around me had recently suffered a painful, life-altering loss. One couple had lost their son, who was killed in the line of duty as a sheriff's deputy in our city. One man, a senior staff member of our church, lost his wife after a long battle with cancer. And another couple had lost their son in a tragic car accident. In all three cases, these grief-stricken people stood there with arms raised toward heaven and hearts turned toward the Lord. It wasn't that they'd been able to lay down their grief themselves as they came into the presence of God. It was that by coming into the presence of their loving Father, their grief, for the moment, had been contextualized with faith, hope, joy.

In the same way that the apostle Simon Peter could stay steady while walking on water as he trained his eyes on Christ,[2] as we train our eyes on Jesus in worship, we find strength like we've never known. This is why we stretch and strain and yearn. This is why we fix our gaze. This is why we reach past earthly distractions. This is why we look to him. We do these things because we cannot be *who we are in Christ* apart from a *divine encounter with Christ*.

We cannot be gracious, apart from an encounter with Grace himself.

We cannot be generous, apart from an encounter with Generosity himself.

We cannot be compassionate, apart from an encounter with Compassion himself.

We cannot be loving, apart from an encounter with Love himself.

Our fragrance cannot overcome the stench of the world, apart from the aroma of Christ.

And so we come. We yearn. We reach. We strain. We *insist* on that life-giving stream. We do these things as demonstrations of our understanding that God doesn't want to top the list of things that we worship; rather, *he wants to* be *the list*. And that to live this way—with God as *the list*—is to live as that which we already are.

9

Plugged In

We Can Demonstrate Remarkable Power

To what will you look for help if you will not look to that which is stronger than yourself?

C. S. LEWIS

The question that may be surfacing in your mind is "All this sounds great—surrendering in worship and releasing myself to who I already am and yearning for spiritual water that can truly satisfy—but how am I supposed to actually do these things? How do I deny the other yearnings and cravings in my life?"

Although the text doesn't state it explicitly, we see in the apostle Paul's remarks to the church at Corinth a real wrestling in their hearts and minds. As we've already seen demonstrated, Corinth was a culture hungry for power—political power, military power, sexual power, and more—and believers there fought the constant temptation to become part of the power structure instead of fight against it. Paul was the most influential apostle the church had ever known, and thus his reputation preceded his arrival into Corinth. Believers there must have expected him to walk with a little more swagger and to throw his weight around a little more often because in the first part of 1 Corinthians, he makes eight robust references to where power is truly found.

- He explains that he came not in the power of "clever speech" but rather in the power of the cross. (See 1 Corinthians 1:17-18.)
- He explains that God was choosing, through Paul, to use things the world considered foolish to shame those who thought they were wise so that nobody would be able to boast in the presence of God. (See 1 Corinthians 1:27–29.)
- He explains that he intentionally avoided lofty language and employed preaching that was "very plain" so that believers in Corinth would trust "not in human wisdom but in the power of God." (See 1 Corinthians 2:1–5.)
- He explains that whenever he was among "mature believers," he employed wisdom not belonging to the world but wisdom that is "the mystery of God" so that together "we can know the wonderful things God has freely given us." (See 1 Corinthians 2:6–7, 12.)
- He explains that whenever he was addressing those who were immature in their faith, those who still stooped to jealousy and quarreling, he spoke to them as though they were still belonging "to this world," feeding them "with milk, not with solid food," because they weren't

quite ready for anything stronger. (See 1 Corinthians 3:1–3.)

- He explains that any growth those young believers did enjoy came not by human effort, but by God, who "makes the [spiritual] seed grow." (See 1 Corinthians 3: 4–7.)
- He explains that to think oneself "wise by this world's standards" is "foolishness to God." (See 1 Corinthians 3:18–19.)
- He explains that, since all anyone has comes from the hand of God, the only thing any believer has to boast about is the Lord. (See 1 Corinthians 3:7, 10–13.)

"The kingdom of God is not just a lot of talk; it is living by God's power," Paul summarized. "Which do you choose? Should I come to you with a rod to punish you, or should I come with love and a gentle spirit?" (1 Corinthians 4:20–21). Such penetrating comments Paul makes throughout, and all of them pointed at one theme: *The most powerful power the world will ever know can't compute in mere human minds.*

I live in a military town that is home to both Army and Air Force installations, and on occasion I'll speak to our servicemen and servicewomen there. On a visit to Fort Carson, an Army base on the south side of town, a young captain from Chicago offered to give me a tour of the base's renowned Sherman tank division. As we neared the parking lot where perhaps four hundred tanks stood motionless, the captain looked at me, looked at those tanks, and said, "Isn't that the saddest thing you've ever seen?"

I was confused. "What do you mean?" I asked, to which he said, "All those tanks, parked when they should be in battle . . ."

I couldn't have disagreed more. "Let me give you a different perspective," I said. "As a pastor, there's no better place for those tanks to be than parked here in this lot. What I feel when I look at those hundreds of tanks is elation, not sadness, because it means they're not off somewhere killing people."

The captain looked at me like I'd grown a third eye. His training had informed a particular posture toward power and strength and might, and my mind was with Paul, who was saying to the church at Corinth essentially this: *You think power comes by way of political prowess or military might, by sexual conquest or by racking up gods to whom you can pray. In fact, it comes by way of Jesus, by his Spirit, by* power from on high. Paul knew that we as believers can't fight our way into people's spiritual imaginations with sheer force, that we can't wedge ourselves in there with human wisdom or wit. He knew that at some point there would need to be a demonstration of God's Spirit in our lives if we were to magnetize people to the cause of Christ.

The instructions he had given them regarding equality, worship, marriage, and sex simply could not be carried out apart from God's power having its way. And yet, based on the sheer volume of references to this power at work in their lives, he recognized that those believers weren't especially excited to cede control of their lives to God.

In this way we're much like the Corinthian church. We rather like the illusion of having complete agency over our own lives. We like to feel in power. We like to seem in control. We like to occupy the driver's seat, even as the insistence will eventually cause us to crash. We like to have our tanks. C. S. Lewis perfectly summed up Paul's certain astonishment over the Corinthians' illogical approach to life in the question that I opened this chapter with: "To what will you look for help if you will not look to that which is stronger than yourself?"[1]

The first non-ministry job I secured following my graduation from Louisiana Tech University was that of a reporter for a local radio station in Shreveport that specialized in chasing storms. I didn't know that this was an actual specialty until I showed up for work and was made to sit for three days straight in a class titled Safety Training for Storm Chasers. There was not only a specialty for such pursuits but also a certification, which seventy-two hours later I proudly earned. Soon enough, my knowledge would be put to the test.

It would go down in northwest Louisiana history as an "epic night" because of the dozen-plus twisters that touched down within the boundaries of our station's listening area, and I was there, in my beater with balding tires, chasing them all. My escapades began at Caddo Lake, where I watched tornadoes skip across the water for what felt like hours. From inside of my car, I fed live reports back to the radio show host, explaining what I was seeing; what it felt like to be *this close* to the storm cells; and, based on the rain and the clouds and the winds, what I expected would happen next. It was exhilarating—for me, at least. Poor Pam, my wife of fewer than six months, was stuck at home listening to the radio, more fretful with each report that I filed.

A report came through my headset that a live tornado was twisting its way northwest of Shreveport, bound for a tiny town called Vivian, which was situated just up Highway 1 between Black Bayou Lake and the Texas state line. Emboldened by my successful work thus far—"Keep after 'em, Brady!" the station manager had encouraged me. "You're doing great out there!"—I pointed my vehicle toward Vivian and raced to catch the storm. What I didn't realize as I entered downtown Vivian was that the storm had stalled and was now behind me; instead of me chasing it, it was chasing me. There had been no training for tornado *catching*.

"Brady Boyd, here in downtown Vivian," I said to the host, who had turned to me for a report. And then the storm was upon me. The swirling winds became violent, ripping giant limbs from nearby trees and cartwheeling them like weightless kindling across my windshield. I eased to the side of the road, terrified to get out of my car. I knew that I would probably die there unless I left my car behind and jumped into the low-lying drainage ditch that sat adjacent to the road. But my judgment was impaired by my perpetually inflated ego that up until this unfortunate moment had been boasting, *I am amazing at this! I was* born *to chase storms!* And so I stayed there in the driver's seat of a car that was dramatically rocking back and forth, determined to file my report.

"Brady?" I heard the host say, his voice dripping with enthusiasm over having an on-the-ground reporter as the storm made its way into town. "Brady Boyd, you're in Vivian *right now,* aren't you?"

During the months leading up to my first day of work at the station, I had worked very hard to perfect my "radio voice," but upon opening my mouth to respond to the host's question, the sounds that emerged were those of a prepubescent schoolboy. "It's . . . so . . . scary!" I heard myself say. *What am I doing?* I scolded myself. *I can't say that!*

For two eternal minutes I chirped and cracked my way through my eyewitness account, trying in vain to clear my throat and regain my composure. The circumstances were winning, and I knew it. I was way out of my league.

The storm eventually passed, and for the next two hours I picked my way through littered roads back to the station. I walked into the offices, where all the crusty old radio veterans waited with bated breath. "It's . . . so . . . scary!" they said in unison, and then they fell apart in waves of laughter. I knew that staying in my car (and not bailing into the ditch like I should have) just to be "the guy" to file the report was a foolish decision, and I hated how foolishness felt.

It would have been bad enough if that storm-chasing mishap had been the only foolishness I knew during that era of my life. It wasn't. The arrogance and impulsivity I demonstrated that night were representative of a deeper problem in my life. Technically, I was a Christ follower, a choice I'd made at age twenty-one. I was also involved in ministry, helping at church with local outreach and youth. But evidently I wasn't yet ready to hand over complete control of my life.

We like to feel in power.

We like to seem in control.

We like to occupy the driver's seat.

I had something of a quick temper. I could be a gunslinger with my words. I was impatient and self-promoting. I satisfied rampant lust online. I wanted my cake and to eat it, too, spiritually speaking: yes, I wanted Jesus, but not like I wanted my other wants.

Still, I had made this "full-surrender" spiritual decision, and so I continued to live with one foot in the Jesus camp and one foot in the camp of the world.

I tried to make a practice of reading my Bible each morning, and one of the passages that always made me cringe is James 1:19–22: "You must all be quick to listen, slow to speak, and slow to get angry. Human anger does not produce the righteousness God desires. So get rid of all the filth and evil in your lives, and humbly accept the word God has planted in your hearts, for it has the power to save your souls.

"But don't just listen to God's word. You must do what it says." That part really made me recoil.

James was directing his comments to his brothers and sisters in Christ, people who had decided to "go God's way" with their lives and who wanted to be whole and holy, set apart for God's good works. And yet something was holding them back, the very same thing that held me back. It's the thing that keeps us from living remarkable lives.

I can still see myself sitting at the little breakfast table in the cramped kitchen of our starter home there in Shreveport, my Bible open to James 1, my head in my hands, my heart in my throat. It was as if I were breathing in the Scriptures through intention but refusing to breathe them out with action, which is about as ludicrous as taking a huge inhale of air and then trying to hold that breath the rest of the day. My face didn't turn blue, but my soul sure did. I wanted to grow up. I wanted to mature in my faith. I wanted to practice what I said I believed. But day after day in my early twenties, I struggled to do these things. It is commonly held that Indian activist Mahatma Gandhi, when asked by a missionary to resolve the apparent discrepancy of so often quoting the words of Jesus while being wholly unwilling to become one of Jesus' followers, said, "Oh, I don't reject Christ. I love your Christ. It's just that so many of you Christians are so unlike your Christ."[2]

This is what James was getting at when he said, "Don't just listen to God's word . . . you must do what it says."

Fine, James, but back to this chapter's opening question: *How do we get that done?*

In my role at New Life, I often ask newcomers what they think about the person of Christ—whether they believe in him, whether they like him, whether they've ever chosen to surrender their lives to him—and in response many say something to the effect of "I've never really been into religion, but I'm a very spiritual person."

This answer makes sense to me, because I spent a lot of

years in that same boat. From my early teenage years until I was twenty-one, I firmly believed that I could chart my own course to God. I chose the wisdom of my own ways over the wisdom of his, and I paid a steep price as a result. I had daily input from the Scriptures. I had smart pastors to look up to. I had parents who loved me and modeled good things for me. And still I refused to be wise. I didn't need God—at least, not in the way he encouraged me to need him. I didn't need the Bible's harsh restrictions. I didn't need two thousand years of church history. I was *bright*. I could *think*. I *knew* stuff—or so I thought.

This all fell into place for me one morning when, at that tiny kitchen table, Bible open, I read for the umpteenth time the words I mentioned earlier from 1 Corinthians 3:18: "Stop deceiving yourselves," Paul said. "If you think you are wise by the world's standards, you need to become a fool to be truly wise."

Well, if foolishness was indeed the first step to becoming wise, then maybe I wasn't as bad off as I thought.

At the same time that I took that broadcasting job in Amarillo, Texas, I remember pushing back intensely against God. I was in complete control of my life—or so I thought, anyway—and I wasn't all that interested in where he wanted things to go. Especially if his desires centered on my reentering the ministry. I had suffered spiritual abuse at the hands of a "professional pastor," I had exhausted myself in my efforts to serve, and I was done with the dysfunction so often prevalent in the local church. I was willing to pick up stakes and move. I was willing to take on a totally new role in radio. I was willing to see where this vocational shift would lead. What I was *not* willing to do was become a pastor. I'd have rather died than follow that course.

But then came my visit to a church in Amarillo called Trinity Fellowship. For the first time in my life, I saw what a "healthy" church could be. I experienced fresh encounters with the Holy Spirit that made me long for more. Most impactful, I met people who *actually lived out the beliefs they said they held*. Remarkable.

This community of believers I happened upon in dusty West Texas had somehow discovered a means for going God's way instead of their own—and, to make things more astounding still, they were doing so with joy. They weren't itchy with dissatisfaction. They weren't puffed up with self-focused pride. They were patient. They were kind. They had carved out a carefully protected space in their schedule so that they could respond to people in need. They trusted God in ways that I clearly did not.

The more I hung around those remarkable people, the more intrigued and inquisitive I became. Over countless mugs of hot coffee, these guys held veritable counseling sessions for me, helping me work through the pain I'd endured, the exhaustion I'd felt, the confusion over how to walk well with Christ. They listened patiently and asked good questions; they regarded me as a friend instead of as a problem they needed to fix. And in the end they helped me discover my core problem, which was a straightforward struggle for power. "You're a sharp young man," I remember Garvin McCarrell saying to me, "but you're not near as sharp as God."

I would soon learn that if I had taken even a fraction of the energy I'd poured into gaining distance from God and invested it in relying more fully on him, I would not have wound up in the predicament I was in—weary, jaded, distracted, full of demands. I would have been plugged into proper power. I would have been operating from a place of divine strength. We can live *independently of* God, or we can live *in dependence on* God. But only one path will lead us to peace—and goodness, and gentleness, and joy.

What began coincidentally with my meeting Garvin in the lobby of Trinity Fellowship would lead me along a path I've now been on for thirty years and counting, a path toward ever-increasing integrity in my walk with Christ. Step by step, I would make sense of the stuff that had vexed me, such as finally coming to grips with what the apostle Paul meant in 1 Corinthians when he exhorted would-be wise people to first become fools. One wisdom-filled friend explained it to me this way: "Brady, the first step in obtaining wisdom is admitting that you are not its source."

I would pick up revolutionary practices that helped me to thrive in everyday life. One of the most meaningful involved asking a simple question at the end of every day. Based on my answer to this singular question, I would know whether I had relied more on my own strength or on God's strength that day. The question was this: Did the solutions I arrived at today reflect the Spirit, or not?

It seems so obvious that it is worth asking, doesn't it? But it wasn't until I started forcing myself to ask and answer that question each evening that I realized how totally self-reliant I'd become. For example, if I'd made a financial decision, had it occurred to me to pause and seek God first? If I'd said yes or no to a particular opportunity, had I checked in with the Holy Spirit, or just plowed ahead using my own rationale? Most times, I had to admit, I'd simply plowed ahead. But if I wasn't the source of all wisdom, then was it wise to "go with my gut"?

The first step in obtaining wisdom is admitting that you are not its source.

If there is one aspect to following Jesus that I struggle with still today, some twenty-five years after that revelation, it is this human-nature tendency to drift toward our own whims and ways. This is a completely understandable phenomenon, seeing as there is *a lot* of brilliance in our world. Someone came up with running water, right? And electricity, and computers, and heat. Someone thought up the Internet. Someone built the first SUV. In every industry imaginable—home building, finance, the culinary arts, medicine, political science, deep-sea fishing, and a thousand more—somebody thought up the original structure, and multiple somebodies after that kept thinking, kept working, kept improving on things from there. As a result, "subject-matter experts" came onto the scene: those who know it, who live it, who love it, who write books about it, who consult on it, who go on speaking tours about it—whatever their distinctive "it" happens to be.

They are *sharp.*

And yet, not as sharp as God.

I find it interesting that the group to whom the apostle Paul issued the warning about "becoming wise by the standards of this age" was filled to overflowing with *super-sharp folks.* This was Corinth, after all, wasteland turned retirement resort for Rome's most skilled military force, led by the inimitable Julius Caesar. This was Corinth, now home to wealthy businessmen, who considered the city a strategic site. This was Corinth, land of opportunity and pleasure—by all standards, the place to be. And it was to these Corinthian people that Paul mailed his missive, a note cautioning them against the very things they were already falling prey to: hedonism, self-interest, worldly gain. It's as though Paul were saying, *It's* wonderful *that you've rebuilt your city, which a hundred years ago lay in ruins. It's* amazing *that businesses are thriving again, and that you're this modern marvel of economic vitality for all the world to see. It's* so cool *that you're so prosperous, and that all that you want you now have. But listen, Corinthians, please listen to me: life is so much more than these things!*

Paul knew that the greatest challenge to following God is believing that we *are* God. Remember step one to obtaining wisdom? It's admitting that we are not its source; it's admitting that we are mere fools. When you and I defer to human wisdom, elevating the wisdom of the world above what God says is true, we deny God his rightful place as the *Creator of wisdom itself*. Cast in that ray of light, it seems ludicrous that, when faced with a decision of any consequence, we would surrender ourselves to a well-meaning friend, a self-help book, even a sharp pastor we know and trust, before surrendering ourselves to our heavenly Father, who holds all knowledge in the palm of his hand. This is the aha that came to me repeatedly as I began to ask myself that end-of-day question: Am I more often plugging into the power of heaven that's available to me, or are my actions betraying the fact that I'm committed to life without God? It was then that I paid closer attention to how God imparts wisdom to those who love him—namely, by his Holy Spirit.

When Paul first came to the Corinthians, he chose not to use "lofty words and impressive wisdom" to tell them God's secret plan (1 Corinthians 2:1) but rather came to them "in weakness—timid and trembling" (v. 3). He spoke plainly. Why? According to verse 5, so that they "would trust not in human wisdom but in the power of God."

Later in that same chapter, we learn that this "power of God"—the Holy Spirit—is the only one who knows and can impart to us the mind of God: "No one can know a person's thoughts except that person's own spirit," the text reads, "and no one can know God's thoughts except God's own spirit. And we have received God's Spirit (not the world's spirit), so we can know the wonderful things God has freely given us" (1 Corinthians 2:11–12). And what *are* those freely given things? A few that hit very close to home:

Peace . . . perfect peace, the remarkable absence of rage.

Purity. Finally, freedom from pornography's rule.

Wisdom. As in, full-on *mind-of-God* wisdom. Isn't that what we're all after: to know that we're getting life right? How I longed to quit playing the fool. How I longed to live as the wise.

Of course, there were dozens of other gifts: salvation itself is a divine gift of God, as is the ability to forgive. Our health is a gift. Our righteousness is a gift. The fact that we can be tempted but not fall into sin—that's an *unspeakable* gift. *All* of life is a gift, if we choose to see it that way, if we approach truth in its fog-free state. God's graciousness is behind every good thing; his Spirit empowering us and guiding us according to that noble work.

Looking back, I could see that while I had made the decision to surrender my life to Jesus at age twenty-one, thus plugging into divine power, so many of my choices from that point forward essentially served to unplug me from that Source. I couldn't consider others' needs when I was consumed by my whims and desires. I couldn't love well when I was using my words as weapons. I couldn't practice faithfulness to my wife when I was bathing in a computer screen's blue light. I couldn't live a life of power in *any* regard when I was walking around unplugged.

It would become something of a mantra for me, this idea of *staying plugged in*. Whenever I realized that I'd reverted to operating in my own strength, I would take a deep breath, literally relax my hands as a figurative releasing of control, and pray, *Father, help me stay plugged in*. The apostle Paul knew that this was our lot in life, that the days indeed are "evil," which is why following his time in Corinth he advised believers to continuously "be filled with the Holy Spirit" (Ephesians 5:18). That simple act of asking for and receiving divine power helped me learn to overcome fear, to make wise decisions, and to keep an eternal perspective as I approached life on this temporal earth. It has helped me learn to live a life of impact, just as those Acts 2 believers did. And it promises to do the same for you, if you're ready not only to get plugged in but also to *stay* plugged into this unparalleled power Source.

Soon after I accepted the senior pastor position at New Life Church, I saw clearly that my work to relinquish day-to-day control to God was paying off, courtesy of trying to manage the large debt load I inherited when I said yes to coming to the church. The church had built a new sanctuary several years prior, funded almost exclusively by bank financing. Now my leadership team and I had to sort out both how we would repay that $26 million loan and how we would cover our monthly mortgage amount until that day, which ran upward of $150,000.

I remember looking at our financial statements my first week on the job, thinking, *There is no way these numbers will work*. Looking back on it now, almost exactly one decade later, I see ironic similarities between that twister I covered in the town of Vivian and New Life's financial free fall of 2007. Both situations were causing unspeakable amounts of destruction.

Both situations were terrifying enough to bring out my prepubescent self. Both situations made me want to run for the nearest ditch and hide out until the worst of the storm passed. But there was one thing that was altogether different from ten years ago when I'd experienced Louisiana's "epic night." The difference was me.

Upon sitting with New Life's financial reality for several weeks and suffering through countless *Oh, God* wrung-hands moments, it occurred to me that I had a choice in the matter: I could either continue fretting, or else I could activate the full strength of my faith, which had been growing and deepening for quite some time. I remembered what it felt like in my car back in Vivian as the sky turned eerily green and the winds began to howl, and I wanted nothing to do with that. I didn't want *this* storm to have its way with me. I wanted to live out what I said I believed.

That day marked the last time I fretted over church finances. That was it: I was done devoting energy to hypotheticals and worry and fear. Immediately, I shifted my prayers from a fear-stricken *Oh, God!* to a faith-building *Okay, God*. It was a much better way to begin.

Okay, God, this is our situation. I know you're aware of it. How can I serve your purposes in this mess?

Okay, God, I choose to trust in your provision. I refuse to scurry around trying in desperation to make ends meet.

Okay, God, I know you're at work here. What are you after, Father? How can I be of help?

Okay, God saved me a lot of time worrying. *Okay, God* helped me to roll up my sleeves.

During one such prayer time, I mentioned to God (seemingly for the millionth time) that I didn't want to cower in fear over this money thing and that I wanted to lead New Life's congregation with passion and vision, not with anxiety and regret. *"I want to dream past the end of the month, God"*—those were the exact words that I said, to which I sensed a divine reply: *"I want that for you too. Build a Dream Center, Brady. As you serve my people in need in your city, the people of New Life will pay off the debt."*

This went against everything I believed and practiced regarding money. Money guru Dave Ramsey himself would have protested this line of thought. Sign up for a massive and costly endeavor when you're up to your eyeballs in debt? This was financial heresy, and I knew it. But I also knew that I'd heard from the Lord.

I took the prompting I'd received to our next elders' meeting and asked the others in the room to prayerfully consider what I believed we were supposed to do. We were supposed to open the Dream Centers of Colorado Springs, to include a free health clinic for underinsured women, a transitional home for homeless moms and their kids, and a neighborhood outreach program in one of our city's most vulnerable communities. And we were supposed to do these things *while we were still in debt.*

In 2011 the women's clinic opened and to date has seen more than five thousand patients who otherwise would have gone without care; in 2015, Mary's Home opened, immediately taking twenty-seven homeless moms and their children off the streets and giving them safety, food security, community, job training, spiritual guidance, and hope; and in 2016 the Adopt-a-Block program took root in south Colorado Springs—all of which happened at the same time that our church reduced our debt load by more than $10 million.

Divine wisdom said, *Don't camp out in despair and anxiety, Brady. Dream of a brighter day ahead.*

Divine wisdom said, *Go ahead and dream. As your church serves, their priorities will shift. They will develop the* longing *to give.*

Divine wisdom said, *You don't have to live in fear any longer. I'm for you. I'm with you. I'm here.*

I don't know what storm seems to be chasing you today. Maybe it's depletion in your marriage, or in your physical body, or in your bank account. Maybe it's the addiction you believe you can't kick. What I do know is this: if you will push pause on your natural reactions—fretting, fuming, wringing your hands, lamenting to a loved one, playing out hypothetical horror stories in your mind—and simply check in with God first, you will find shelter in your storm. Romans 8:26 says that the "Holy Spirit helps us in our weakness" and that when we don't know what God wants us to pray for, the Holy Spirit "prays for us with groanings that cannot be expressed in words."

God knows that when the sky turns green and the winds start howling, we're too freaked out to know *what* to pray. Rest assured that when you're stuck and scared and unsure of how to move forward, you can simply turn those truths into your prayer. *God, I'm stuck. And scared. And unsure of how to go on . . .* And then let the Holy Spirit take things from there.

What I'm saying is that when you and I surrender ourselves fully to God, from that point forward, we've got *God praying to God* on our behalf. God will get us unstuck. He will infuse our impotence with his strength. And then he will empower us to live truly remarkable lives, as we minister to others in need.

Here's what you can expect upon coming to God with even a feeble prayer: As you sit in his presence and allow his Spirit to intercede on your behalf, translating and beseeching and communicating with spiritual groans, you will move beyond your natural thoughts. You will go beyond your natural imagination. You will pass your natural reasoning. And joyously, gratefully, blissfully, finally, you will be divinely directed as to what to do next.

We are given not only divine discernment regarding how to persist through the storm we're in, but also the *supernatural strength* to put legs to that discernment. In other words, not only does the Spirit help us know better, he helps us *do* better too.

Which brings me to the second of the Holy Spirit's interventions in the life of a believer: we are given not only divine discernment regarding how to persist through the storm we're in, but also the *supernatural strength* to put legs to that discernment. In other words, not only does the Spirit help us know better, he helps us *do* better too.

When we seek first the kingdom of God instead of seeking first the wisdom of the world, we are provided divine discernment for making wise decisions, for caring for people, for honoring God. We begin manifesting what Paul called "the fruit" of the Spirit, those things that become evident in our lives whenever we plug into God's power source instead of our own. "Let the Holy Spirit guide your lives," Paul told the believers at Galatia. "Then you won't be doing what your sinful nature craves. The sinful nature wants to do evil, which is just the opposite of what the Spirit wants. And the Spirit gives us desires that are the opposite of what the sinful nature desires. These two forces are constantly fighting each other, so you are not free to carry out your good intentions" (Galatians 5:16–17).

When, then, does the "sinful nature" crave? Paul went on. "When you follow the desires of your sinful nature," he said, "the results are very clear: sexual immorality, impurity, lustful pleasures, idolatry, sorcery, hostility, quarreling, jealousy, outbursts of anger, selfish ambition, dissension, division, envy, drunkenness, wild parties, and other sins like these. Let me tell you again, as I have before, that anyone living that sort of life will not inherit the Kingdom of God" (vv. 19–21).

The Spirit wants far different things. "The Holy Spirit," Paul confirmed, "produces this kind of fruit in our lives: love, joy, peace, patience, kindness, goodness, faithfulness, gentleness, and self-control. There is no law against these things!" (Galatians 5:22–23).

Did the solutions I arrived at today reflect the Spirit, or not? What a useful question that is. Think of it: you find yourself angered by something your spouse says to you and decide to fire back with a winning shot. Did the solution reflect the Spirit, or not?

Or you are tempted to "just round up" on your expense report—not by pennies but by hundreds, it turns out. But everyone at the company does it, and the company doesn't care. At least, nobody is ever called out. Did the solution you came to reflect the Spirit, or not?

Or you blow it with your kid and ground him from now till kingdom come. You know you can't stand by the punishment you doled out, but you're not about to tell *him* that. Spirit-directed solution, or something else entirely? Only you, before God, can know.

Before I depress you any further with sinking examples, let me share a secret: the more faithful you and I are to ask and answer this question each day, the less frequent our cringes will be. As we are faithful to get before God each day and review the solutions we came to, we will open lines of communication that have been blocked. We'll discover that, when faced with even a trivial decision—where should I eat? which couch should I buy? what on earth should I say?—we'll check in with God for advice. And when the big decisions roll around, such as how to resolve deep conflict, how to discipline our children, and how to forgive the one who caused pain, we'll find we're *already plugged into the power we need* to wisely make the choice.

> *Did the solutions I arrived at today reflect the Spirit, or not?* Let me share a secret: the more faithful you and I are to ask and answer this question each day, the less frequent our cringes will be.

10

A Foretaste of What's to Come

We Can Hold Fast to Remarkable Hope

You will argue with yourself that there is no way forward. But with God, nothing is impossible. He has more ropes and ladders and tunnels out of pits than you can conceive.[1]

JOHN PIPER

It is exciting and empowering to be reminded of the possibilities in life for we who are fully surrendered to the Holy Spirit's power instead of our own. We can *know* better. We can *do* better. We can bear timely, useful fruit. We can be a kinder, gentler, smarter, sturdier version of ourselves, one governed by that which is *supernatural* instead of what is heard, what is felt, what is seen. But as great as this life-that-is-truly-life earthbound reality is, I have better news for you still: the divinely empowered existence will one day be our permanent state. This was part of the news that the apostle Paul wished to convey to the believers gathered at Corinth after his departure, as evidenced by his words in his third and final letter to them.

"It is God who enables us, along with you, to stand firm for Christ," he wrote in 2 Corinthians 1:21–22. "He has commissioned us, and he has identified us as his own by placing the Holy Spirit in our hearts as the first installment that guarantees everything he has promised us."

Jesus' promise that complete transformation would work its way in our lives, that in him we would never die, that death ultimately would be swallowed up in victory—these and scores more assurances, Paul was saying, *began to see their fulfillment* with the Holy Spirit's arrival into our lives. The apostle referred to this power as a "first installment"—a down payment, if you will . . . a foretaste of what was to come.

The divinely empowered existence will one day be our permanent state.

Pam and I took a weeklong vacation recently, and as part of the online reservation process for the rental property where we hoped to stay, I was asked to supply a credit card or debit card number so that the owners of that property could charge a portion of the overall rental ahead of time. That smaller amount—the down payment—was a signal to them that I was good for the money, that there was more where that came from, and that upon the completion of our agreement—in this case, Pam and me staying in their home—I would joyfully hand over the larger amount as payment in full.

I think also about the change in seasons. Here in Colorado, winters can be extremely cold . . . or they are to this transplanted Southerner, anyway. Every March or April, when I see that first green bud pop through my snow-covered flower beds as one did that day I was on the phone, I think, *Ahh. Spring. It's coming again this year.* The delight I feel over that singular bud is multiplied exponentially several weeks later when trees are in full bloom.

It is something that points to something else: a down payment, a foretaste, an installment . . . a promise of grandeur to come. *This* is what the Acts 2 indwelling of the Holy Spirit in believers' minds and hearts and lives was intended to be, a hint of heavenly bliss. "No eye has seen, no ear has heard, and no mind has imagined," Paul wrote to those believers, "what God has prepared for those who love him."

Greater power than we know today is just around the bend. We ain't seen nothin' yet.

I want to step back for a moment and acknowledge why Paul's reminder that we looked at earlier from 2 Corinthians 1:21–22 carried such weight. Paul didn't want those believers to forget that they belonged to God, and that the Spirit living inside of them was proof of the purchase he'd made. Further, he wanted them to remember that the Spirit—with all his guidance, direction, and divine power—was but a "first installment" of something to come. With those words, Paul was infusing the Corinthian believers with *hope*. He was saying, *Don't cave to today's circumstances. Let the promise of tomorrow's blessings see you through.*

And what, exactly, were those "blessings of tomorrow"?

In 1 Corinthians, Paul spent a full fifty-eight verses explaining why believers in Christ can have hope, despite the challenges life dares to present. You can read the entire text for yourself in 1 Corinthians 15; for now, a few highlights will do: "Let me now remind you, dear brothers and sisters, of the Good News I preached to you before . . . ," Paul said. "It is this Good News that saves you if you continue to believe the message I told you—unless, of course, you believed something that was never true in the first place" (1 Corinthians 15:1–2). Paul then puts words to that Good News: Christ died for our sins. He was buried and rose from the dead. He was seen by more than five hundred eyewitnesses at one time. Yes, the end will come, but believers? They'll live on.

What Paul endeavored to do in his lengthy reminder to the Corinthian church was to lift their sights from that which they thought could fulfill them to that which truly would. Jaded by the wayward culture surrounding them, those believers were beginning to think that success in life looked like social acceptance, sexual satisfaction, military prowess, and the freedom to do as they pleased—all trends that ring familiar to our modern-day ears. Paul said, in essence, these things—*all* things—will be humbled beneath the feet of Jesus Christ.

The Corinthian audience would have known well what Paul meant. In those days in the Middle East, one of the most offensive things you could have done was to show another person the soles of your feet.[2] This was a contemptuous gesture on par with no other, representing domination, conquest, control. It was the equivalent of standing over a person who was lying on the ground, putting your shoe on that person's throat, and gloating. "This is the picture I want you to have in mind," Paul was saying, "of where all earthly indulgences that take the place of Christ in your mind and heart are headed."

Rampant self-sufficiency will be humbled beneath Jesus' feet.

Lustfulness and drunkenness will be humbled beneath Jesus' feet.

Abuse of people and abuse of power will be humbled beneath Jesus' feet.

Marital infidelity will be humbled beneath Jesus' feet.

Sexual promiscuity will be humbled beneath Jesus' feet.

Every sin of *every* kind will be humbled beneath Jesus' feet, as well as the sinners who happen to be committing those sins. So, "stop sinning," Paul declared in 1 Corinthians 15:34. Quit clinging to that which destroys you, and hold fast to that which brings life. *Put your hope only in Christ, for in Christ, alone, can hope be found.*

Last summer, Pam and the kids and I were given tickets to a Colorado Rockies game. I had never seen the Rockies play; what's more, that day they were playing my Texas Rangers, the team that during my growing-up years was the closest pro team around. Despite my family's protests—"It's August! It's hot! We'll fry to death!"—I ushered them all toward the car one afternoon and took off toward metro Denver.

It was a pretty sticky afternoon, as it turned out, and I could tell within thirty minutes of arrival that we were in for a long day. Our seats were getting a direct hit of sunshine, there was no breeze to speak of, and you can slurp only so many frozen lemonades before all that simple syrup makes your stomach turn. By the fifth inning, I could feel my face getting crispy; by the sixth inning, all four of us were dripping with sweat; by the eighth inning, Pam was feeling faint.

The Texas Rangers had been on something of a streak, but in this game all was lost. We were down five to one, the Rockies were on fire, and we couldn't do anything right. We looked like a Little League team out there; I was making my family suffer for *this*? After the eighth inning, I looked at my withered wife and sunburned children and said, "Let's bail."

We made our way out of the stadium and across the massive set of parking lots to our car, wove our way out of the complex, found the road we needed, and headed out. My expectations had been low for my team that afternoon, but I couldn't resist turning on the radio and following the rest of the game. When my Rangers scored their first run of the ninth inning, I was surprised. When they scored their second, third, and fourth runs, I was stunned. When they pulled out yet another run in the game's final minutes to take a six-to-five lead, I thought, *I am a horrible, horrible fan.*

In his robust reminder, the apostle Paul was cautioning us against the very same thing. *Jesus is here,* he wanted us to understand. *Jesus is at work. Jesus is up to something big. He is bringing everything to completion. Work in cooperation with those divine efforts, not against them. Hold fast to hope in him until the very end.*

Don't bail.
Don't bail.
Don't bail.

I find it interesting that when believers of old gathered just before the Middle Ages at the Council of Nicaea to crystallize the foundational beliefs of Christianity in the Nicene Creed, they looked to Paul's words in 1 Corinthians 15 for inspiration. The opening of the creed reads:

We believe in one God, the Father, the Almighty,
Maker of heaven and earth, of all that is, seen and unseen.[3]

The themes that Paul highlighted in his plea—creation and redemption and restoration—show up in the creed too. There is a bigger story at work around us, this confession attests. There is more to life than just what we see.

Remarkably, down through the ages this creed has stood the test of time. Christians from every stream of the body of Christ can and do confess these words: Catholic, Protestant, Eastern Orthodox, Lutheran, Reformed, Presbyterian, Baptist, Pentecostal, and more. Were you to visit our north campus in Colorado Springs, you'd find this statement of faith printed in large letters on several of our most visible interior walls. We recite these words and meditate on these words and honor these words because these words help us to remember what we believe. Why we do what we do. Where our hope, ultimately, is found. Essentially, *when you are tempted to leave this game early,* these words declare, *come back to what you know to be true. Have hope. Take heart. Don't bail.*

A dozen years ago I received the phone call every grown child dreads. It was my mom on the line. "Brady," she said through choked-back tears, "your father has been diagnosed with cancer." That one sentence sucked all the air out of my body. She fell quiet, waiting for me to speak, but what was there to say?

For the next three years I prayed more aggressively than I'd ever prayed. I fasted. I begged. I declared. I pled. I did everything I knew to do. And yet my dad slowly died.

After my father's funeral, I headed back to Gateway Church, where I pastored at the time. Following a worship service, I walked to the front of the auditorium, where I stood alongside all the other pastors and leaders who were part of the "prayer team." Each weekend people streamed toward us at the close of every service: people in need of prayer. And we would lay hands on those people, and we would beseech heaven on behalf of those people, and we would impart to those people great hope. I myself needed such things that weekend, and yet I was supposed to pray for others.

As the music played and congregants disbanded, a woman approached me. She was slight of build, she was soft of speech, and her eyes were wet with tears. "I have cancer," she nearly whispered. "Would you pray for me?"

My heart sank in my chest. I had just prayed for three years straight for my dad, and now he was buried six feet underground.

I prayed for that woman, but it wasn't a very bold prayer. In the process of losing my dad, something had been emptied from my soul, something that felt like faith. At the center of my problem was a question: Did I still truly *believe*?

Did I believe that God was willing to comfort me?

Did I believe he was able to?

Did I still believe that Jesus was worth following?

Did I believe that brighter days were ahead?

Those were frustrating, fearful times.

I was watching an episode of *MythBusters* once when Jamie and Adam, the show's affable, geeky hosts, were trying to disprove the myth that elephants were afraid of mice. To test the assertion, the pair traveled to Africa, enlisted the aid of a big-game safari, and constructed a scenario featuring a small herd of elephants coming upon a ball of elephant dung that had been holed out to accommodate a small, white mouse. When the herd reached a certain spot, the ball, which was attached to invisible thread that was being manipulated by a person out of sight, would be flipped upright to reveal the rodent underneath. Predictably, the mouse would scamper across the ground, which then rather surprisingly caused the giant beasts to stop abruptly, reverse direction, and storm off in a frenzy, clearly fearful of what they'd seen.

"Well, what if it's just the movement of the ball and not the mouse inside that frightens them?" one of the hosts asked the other, and so the experiment was run again, this time with no mouse involved. The ball was positioned, the herd was goaded toward it, and as it neared, the ball was flipped. What did the elephants do now? They kept walking, right over the ball, paying no attention whatsoever to the fact that it had just tumbled end over end. "I can't believe that I'm saying this," one of the hosts said in conclusion, "but it turns out that quite unbelievably, elephants *are* afraid of mice."

I thought about that episode for several days after I'd seen it. And about how many times I'd allowed "mice" to send me running away in fear. In the heavenly realm, I must have looked like a complete idiot. Wasn't the power in me greater than that?

I'm guessing you can relate to this idea. What mice have put *you* on the run?

Trouble in your marriage?

The economy?

A rebellious child?

Job insecurity?

A flagging friendship?

A secret you hope doesn't come out?

How about a cancer diagnosis, like the one my dad received years ago?

I've been on an African safari before, and here is what I know: the elephants I saw that day could crush a *thousand* mice. As we neared one herd—a mama and her calf—our guide stopped the Jeep and put the thing in park. All of us bold, brash Americans hollered, "Aw, come on! Can't you get closer than that?"

To which our experienced guide said, "Yes, if you wish to die."

After a rather dramatic pause, the guide then said, "In two swift moves, that cow could crush the whole lot of us like a tin can. This is as far as I'll go."

And yet this is the animal that's afraid of a tiny mouse.

Whenever I think about our tendency to run in fear whenever we get spooked by life, I picture God's angels in heaven looking down on us believers who are trembling in the presence of harmless mice and shaking their heads in wonder, thinking, *What's gotten into them?* So much latent power residing inside of us, so much promise, so much *hope.*

The assurance that Paul was offering those believers in Corinth was that all things are under Christ's feet. *All things,* meaning all . . . things—as in: nothing excluded from the list. Everything, everywhere, in all cases, for all time, *sits under the feet of Christ.* The diseases and the disasters, the preoccupations and the prodigals, the storms and the shattered dreams, the foibles and the failures, the thousand reasons that we fear—*all of it* is under his control. Which means that for now and forever we need not flee at the sight of a mouse. We can choose to cling to hope, not fear, as we make our way through this life.

My dad's death—in the earthly sense, anyway—forced me to reconcile whether I believed God still possessed resurrection power or not. I conceded that he'd raised his Son, Jesus, from the dead, but was he still in that business today?

I wrestled with that question all the way home from my dad's funeral, eventually resolving in my heart that, yes, I still believed. God, through Jesus, really had created all things—my dad among them. Jesus really had come down from heaven to suffer and die for our sake. Jesus really had risen again and now was seated at the right hand of the Father. Jesus really was coming back again to judge the living and the dead. And because of these truths, other truths could be trusted: that I was seen, and known, and loved. Jesus knew the extent of my suffering and promised to not abandon me there. What's more, he had gone to prepare an eternal place for me where death would reign no more.

Yes, my father had passed away. But equally true, he *was not dead*. He had left this reality for another one. He was alive, and he'd been healed.

In the wake of that terrible loss, I remember coming across a story in Scripture that I'd read many times before. Deeply emotional experiences always shift our perspective, and Dad's death had certainly shifted mine. I came to the passage with fresh enthusiasm, eager to learn what I could learn.

The text is found in John 11 and features a man, Lazarus, being raised from the dead. You probably recall that Lazarus and his two sisters, Mary and Martha, were personal friends of Jesus, and so when Lazarus fell ill, the sisters sent word to Jesus to let him know.

He was ministering a few miles away, but instead of hastily making his way to Bethany, where Lazarus and the sisters were, he decided to stay put. Looking at his disciples, he said, "Lazarus's sickness will not end in death. No, it happened for the glory of God so that the Son of God will receive glory from this" (John 11:4).

For three full days, Jesus stayed away, only deciding on the fourth day to head to Lazarus's side. Lazarus's sister Martha was incensed. "Lord," she said, "if only you had been here, my brother would not have died" (v. 21).

To which Jesus replied, "Your brother will rise again," (v. 23).

Martha, being a Jew, assumed Jesus was talking about the end of days, when a final resurrection would occur.[4] Jesus meant something different entirely.

"I am the resurrection and the life," he clarified. "Anyone who believes in me will live, even after dying. Everyone who lives in me and believes in me will never ever die. Do you believe this, Martha?" (vv. 25–26).

Everyone who lives in me and *believes* in me . . .

Do you believe, Martha?

Do you believe, Brady?

Do *any* of us still believe?

Hope is birthed in belief. We cannot hold fast to the hope Jesus promised us if we do not first make the choice to believe.

The most famous part of the story then ensues, of course, involving Jesus raising Lazarus from the dead, and for the first time in all the times I'd read the account, I saw the connection between that miracle and Martha's belief. In answer to Jesus' intimate question—*Do you believe, Martha?*—the woman replied, *I do.* "Yes, Lord," she told him. "I have always believed you are the Messiah, the Son of God, the one who has come into the world from God" (v. 27). A creedal response, you might say. A confirming-foundational-truths response, you might say. A holding-fast-to-hope response, you might say. A perfect response, I say. And upon uttering those words of belief, a miracle unfolding in Martha's midst.

As an aside, have you ever noticed that just after you purchase a vehicle—a Nissan truck, say—hundreds more people do the same? All around you, on your morning commute, in the parking lot of your local grocery store, on the neighborhood roads leading to your house, you see dozens and dozens of Nissan trucks that you'd never noticed before. How uncanny that suddenly everyone has Nissan trucks! What are the chances of *that*?

When Martha laid down her frustration, her anger, her fear, and picked up belief and buoyancy and hope, she witnessed a miracle then and there: that of her brother being raised from the dead. As she fixed her eyes not on her circumstances but on Jesus, she saw Jesus' realm slowly breaking through. The kingdom is coming and yet has not fully arrived; it is here and yet not all the way; it is intersecting and intervening and interjecting and interrupting the natural order of things. It is giving us sneak peeks of the supernatural ties that bind the universe up. It is showing us what *real* reality is like, where *all* things are under Christ's feet.

In the Old Testament, the Hebrew Testament, when the nation of Israel feared that their best days were long behind them and all hope for their future had been lost, God sent a prophet named Ezekiel to encourage their hearts. He gave Ezekiel a word picture and asked the prophet to share it with the Israelites. It was a picture of promise. It was a picture of potential. It was a picture of hope.

By way of geographic context, you might envision a massive valley that descends from tall mountains on both sides. The valley is filled to overflowing with human remains now turned to bone and dust. Whatever act of destruction occurred, it occurred long, long ago. All that is here now is desolation, hopelessness, "what once was."

In Ezekiel 37:1, we find a stirring account of the prophet Ezekiel's vision of "a valley filled with bones." There the Lord asks the prophet if those bones will ever have life in them again. The prophet isn't so sure. Then the Lord tells the prophet to speak to the bones, declaring that they will indeed live again. They will have flesh and muscle and skin again. They will know breath. They will know *life*.

The prophet did as he was told. And not only did those bones rise up, rattling miraculously back to life, but the sum of them formed a great army, determined to do great things.

Spiritually, physically, emotionally, politically, financially—from every angle, it seemed the nation of Israel was dead and gone. All that remained of the once-great kingdom was this valley of broken bones. To all who surveyed this dark, grim scene, the question on their minds was *Where is God in all of this?*

The same question Martha would one day ask: "Where were you, Jesus?"

If only you'd been here, Jesus . . .

If you'd come, my brother could have lived . . .

To which Jesus asks, "Do you believe?"

He knew: All things will one day be under his feet.

Don't bail.

Don't bail.

Don't bail.

Instead, lean in and listen closely. Do you hear those bones rattling to life?

"I know your heart is broken," Jesus says, "but this pain will not end in death."

"I know the fear you feel is terrifying," Jesus says, "but this dread will not end in death."

"I know your addiction is real," Jesus says, "but its pull will not end in death."

"I know the uncertainty is maddening," Jesus says, "but this exasperation will not end in death."

"I know you miss your father," Jesus says, "but this agony will not end in death . . ."

Believe that I am who I say that I am, and that I am doing what I said I would do, and all things will come together again. I will bring you back to life.[5]

Now, we could stop here and walk away heartened by this reminder to believe, to have hope. But you get the sense from the apostle Paul's exhortations to the believers at Corinth to stop sinning, and quit indulging the lusts of these earthly bodies, which "cannot inherit the Kingdom of God," and "think carefully about what is right," and to "know God"—that there is more to hope-filled living than the perspective we maintain in our own minds and hearts, independent of anyone or anything else. You get the feeling that there is more on the line than how we order our own private worlds.

What's on the line, Paul said, is the gospel, the Good News Jesus asked us to spread. Why should we ourselves "risk our lives hour by hour?" he said in 1 Corinthians 15:30. What value is there in "fighting wild beasts . . . if there will be no resurrection from the dead? And if there is no resurrection, 'Let's feast and drink, for tomorrow we die!' " (v. 32).

Why hold fast to hope, in other words, if hope will fail us in the end?

Paul knew that what Jesus had said was true: that there *would* be a resurrection, that believers in Jesus *would* inherit eternal life. And his plea to all who name themselves followers of Christ was to help others embrace these truths too. So we come to this final piece of the "hope" puzzle, which is this: the surest way to see that you're holding on to hope in Christ is that you bring divine hopefulness with you wherever you go. You bring peace to chaos. You bring joy to dismay. You bring clarity to confusion. You bring understanding to fractured bonds. You bring compassion to the struggling. You bring generosity to those who take. You bring light where there's only been darkness. You bring *hope* to a hopeless world.

The surest way to see that you're holding on to hope in Christ is that you bring divine hopefulness with you wherever you go.

I get into trouble every time I mention politics around New Life, but it doesn't stop me from opening my mouth. This very idea that we can spread divine hope to a world that is hopeless is what renders politics impotent at best. I am all for freedom, security, and pothole-free roads, but when we as a people look to our government to fix what ails the human soul, we ask them to overreach into territory where they're not fit to tread, let alone *lead others* along that path. Republicans look at the hurting and helpless and addicted and weak and say, "I got to where I am without any help. Pull yourself up by your bootstraps! Why don't you just fix yourself?" Democrats take in the same lot of folks and say, "Here. I've got a free program for you. It will help with all the superficial stuff, but it won't meet the needs of your soul."

You bring peace to chaos. You bring joy to dismay. You bring clarity to confusion. You bring understanding to fractured bonds. You bring compassion to the struggling. You bring generosity to those who take. You bring light where there's only been darkness. You bring *hope* to a hopeless world.

Do you see the problem here?

In the next chapter we will look at how the church can and must fill this ever-widening gap that politics cannot address, but for now, let me say this: only the hope of Jesus can satisfy the soul that Jesus himself created. Every other attempt we could make is forcing a square peg into a round hole: futile, pointless, unwise.

But again, it's not enough for us to believe this information in our minds and hearts and then carry that belief secretly throughout our lives. Remarkable living demands that there is evidence of something remarkable going on in and through us about which people are compelled to remark. That "something remarkable," in my view, is spreading hope. It's reminding people that this earthbound life is hardly worth living for, because one day it will die.

Only the hope of Jesus can satisfy the soul that Jesus himself created. Every other attempt we could make is forcing a square peg into a round hole: futile, pointless, unwise.

Let's revisit the scene from Lazarus's resurrection in John 11. I intentionally left out a portion of that story earlier that I'd like to cover with you now. In verses 38 through 44, we find the events that preceded Lazarus coming out of the grave:

> *He [Jesus] arrived at the tomb, a cave with a stone rolled across its entrance. "Roll the stone aside," Jesus told them.*
>
> *But Martha, the dead man's sister, protested, "Lord, he has been dead for four days. The smell will be terrible."*
>
> *Jesus responded, "Didn't I tell you that you would see God's glory if you believe?" So they rolled the stone aside. Then Jesus looked up to heaven and said, "Father, thank you for hearing me. You always hear me, but I said it out loud for the sake of all these people standing here, so that they will believe you sent me."Then Jesus shouted, "Lazarus, come out!" And the dead man came out, his hands and feet bound in graveclothes, his face wrapped in a headcloth. Jesus told them, "Unwrap him and let him go!"*

Whenever we tell the story of Lazarus being raised from the dead, we generally attribute 100 percent of the action to Jesus. "Jesus finally went to Bethany." "Jesus called Lazarus forth from the grave." "Jesus raised Lazarus from the dead." And while these statements are indeed true, we mustn't miss the critical role Lazarus's family and friends played that day. As Jesus approached Lazarus's grave, the text says that he instructed those who cared about Lazarus who were gathered there that day to "roll the stone aside."

Now, to state the painfully obvious: Jesus had the ability to roll the stone away himself. This stone would have been massive, most likely weighing one to two tons, and yet he had the ability to roll the stone to *Mars* if he so desired. Why, then, didn't he do it? Why did he ask those onlookers to move the stone?

Around New Life, I've had the opportunity to meet some truly remarkable people. I'm thinking here of a couple who approached me one weekend after I'd given my talk and said, "Pastor Brady, thank you for that message. When we walked in here a couple of hours ago, we were on the verge of getting a separation. We're not going to pursue that anymore. We're going to work at our marriage some more."

I think of a mom who was absolutely fed up with the emotional roller coaster she'd been on with her teenage son and was ready to disown the young man if he didn't shape up. "I realize I'm not faultless in this," she admitted to me one day. "I'm going to extend grace to him and work on my own stuff first, and then see what unfolds from there."

I think of a guy who is part of our college-age group who

had a friend from school who is pretty rough. The friend drinks too much, parties too hard, and has no real use for God, even as the New Life kid prays for his friend, passes books to his friend, and invites his friend to church. He is determined to help his friend come to know Christ and to find greater purpose in life.

I think of a husband and wife who have a neighbor who's a single mom of twin boys. Lately the mom has been making regrettable choices, and while she acts like the consequences she's facing are no big deal, this couple knows she's hurting inside. Instead of casting judgment, this couple and their daughter, who is the same age as those twin boys, make a practice of heading outside on as many evenings as possible to play with those kids and to encourage their mom.

The thing that these and scores more of these *remarkable people* have in common is that they're willing to do some heavy lifting on behalf of people they know. They're willing to roll the stones away, as it were, so that what was dead can be brought to life.

It's possible you are wrestling with a big issue these days. You may be begging God for a resurrection of your marriage. You may be begging God for a resurrection of your relationship with your daughter or son. You may be begging God for a resurrection of your career. You may be begging God for a resurrection of your physical body. Whatever the resurrection involves that you covet most today, my question for you is the same: Will you do some of the heavy lifting that may be required to join in God's redemptive work?

Will you forgive? That can be a wildly heavy task.

Will you reach out? A heavy thing, for sure.

Will you choose love over indictment? Will you lend a hand? Will you pray?

At the moment, I have two friendships that are struggling, and in both cases I share the blame. I feel justified in my distance and in my anger, but that rationale won't get me far. The question I have to ask myself is the same question I asked you: Will I step over my frustration, my justification, my pride, and work to move those stones? Or will I sulk and pout and fume and rage and get nowhere in the end?

This decision isn't based only on the story of Lazarus, as you well know. Throughout Scripture, Jesus speaks scores of exhortations that remind us to *love* and *serve* and *give*. All those "one anothers" in the New Testament aren't there by accident; Jesus expects us to *get them done*.

And then there's this: Once we have worked to help roll the stone away, freeing those inside to taste new life, will we stick around to unwrap their graveclothes for them? Will we help keep that fresh hope alive?

When Lazarus emerged from the tomb, he was wrapped in heavy bandages. As was the day's custom, his dead body had been anointed with oil and spices and essentially mummy-wrapped from head to toe. His hands had been lain over his chest and bound up, his feet had been bound up, his entire frame was bound and secured. So upon hearing Jesus' command to "come forth," it wasn't like he *bolted* out of the grave. Rather, the man probably penguin-stepped his way out. Think of a Texan walking on icy road . . . teeny-tiny steps. Lazarus could barely walk, let alone remedy his bound-up state. "I'm so happy to have found newness of life," Lazarus could have said. "Now, will someone help me go live it?"

When you and I explain the Scriptures to a new believer, we unwrap their graveclothes a little bit more.

When you and I pray expectantly with someone who is sorting out his faith, we unwrap his graveclothes a little bit more.

When you and I are patient and kind with someone who is finally making a recovery, we unwrap her graveclothes a little bit more.

When you and I offer hope to one who is hopeless and then stay put as they find their way, we unwrap their graveclothes once and for all. We help them *live* this new life they've found.

I remember what it was like to be a young man living in darkness who finally saw the light. In the years leading up to 1988, I was a rebellious fool who loved my sin more than my God and who for all intents and purposes lived in a tomb that bore a sealed-shut massive stone. There was no hope for me. There was no future for me. This was no way to live a life.

But then Jesus prompted my mom and a few pastors and a few friends to gather and roll that stone away. Jesus called me forth and gave me new life, and those loved ones pitched in and helped. They invested in me. They prayed for me. They taught me how to live. They anticipated great things for my future, and they taught me to do the same.

After the apostle Paul reminded the believers at Corinth of the foundations of their belief and exhorted them to stop "playing fast and loose with resurrection facts" and instead to "awaken to the holiness of life" (1 Corinthians 15:34, MSG), he gave them a word of encouragement that I'd like to pass to you now. Again from *The Message*, "With all this going for us, my dear, dear friends, stand your ground. And don't hold back. Throw yourselves into the work of the Master, confident that nothing you do for him is a waste of time or effort" (1 Corinthians 15:58).

The time you spend praying for a wayward friend . . .

The effort you put forth in helping a struggling neighbor get back on her feet . . .

The hours you invest teaching a teenager to handle money . . .

The patience you exhibit listening to a loved one's confession . . .

The mediating and serving, the giving and connecting, the grace, the compassion, the love . . .

None of these things is ever in vain. *It is to these efforts that we were called.*

Not long ago, I helped lead a presbytery service at the church in Amarillo where I used to serve. The format of such services is that several pastors are called to the front of the auditorium, where they take turns giving prophetic words of encouragement to various people in the congregation. There's nothing magical about this; you simply lean into the presence of the Holy Spirit, listen for his wisdom as it relates to people's lives, and then share aloud what you hear.

As I go through everyday life, knowing that I will invariably bump into scores of people in a given day, I carry three questions with me—questions that position me to seize opportunities to serve and love and give, to bring hope to hopeless hearts. The questions follow right along with the purpose of prophesy, as Paul delineated in 1 Corinthians 14:3. "One who prophesies," Paul wrote, "*strengthens* others, *encourages* them, and *comforts* them" (emphasis mine). The questions are these:

1. *What can I say to help this person keep going?* This question speaks to the power of establishment. Too many people are ready to give up and give in; I long to help them stay the course.
2. *What has God spoken to this person that I can confirm?* This question speaks to the power of agreement. If God is trying to get through to someone, I want to be part of clearing those airwaves, not adding static to an already noisy scene.
3. *What pain has this person experienced that God wants to comfort?* This question speaks to the power of relief. How might my words reflect the Father's generous compassion? What relief does the Spirit long to provide?

While I was waiting for my turn at that presbytery service, I asked these three questions over and over again. "Father, who needs your strengthening power today? Who needs to be reminded of what you've said? Who needs the comfort of a loving Father this morning? Speak, Lord. I'm listening to you . . ."

My attention fell on a couple in their fifties, I'd guess, whom I'd never met before. I couldn't get a certain prompting out of my mind: *It's their daughter . . . their only daughter . . . Their daughter is coming home . . . I have plans for this child, and for them.*

I went over to the couple and said, "When you get home this afternoon, I want you read Luke 15, the story of the prodigal son. I can't shake the impression that there is a prodigal in your life, and the comfort I want to offer you today is that your daughter is coming home for good. God has plans to prosper her—and you."

As soon as the words left my mouth, both the wife and her husband broke down in tears. Later the story came tumbling out, involving their daughter, a barrel racer, who had left home too young to be part of the rodeo culture. She had fallen in love with a guy who was no good for her, as evidenced by his dumping her shortly thereafter for another woman. Two weeks before that presbytery service, that young lady had shown up on her parents' doorstep, broken and frail and afraid. For *eight years* this girl had been running, but finally she'd found her way home.

Following the service, the young woman came up to me, her parents at her side, and said, "Pastor Brady, I'm the prodigal."

"I've been there too," I said.

I was able to tell her and her parents then and there that God had a plan for them and that his plan was for their *vitality* in him—that his plan for them was *hope*.

I went home that afternoon deeply in awe of the goodness and grace of God. The resurrection power we can know in this life fits us for unparalleled impact and joy. But the better news still is that it's only a preview of the grandeur we'll one day enjoy.

11

Let the River Flow

History Can Declare Us a Remarkable Church

Anyone who is to find Christ must first find the church.

MARTIN LUTHER

Just before Jesus faced his crucifixion, he made a bold declaration to his disciples, Simon Peter among them. The group had arrived in Caesarea Philippi, Matthew 16:13–14 tells us, when Jesus turned to his followers and asked, "Who do people say that the Son of Man is?" The replies Jesus received were quite flattering, if not totally wrong: " 'Well,' they replied, 'some say you're John the Baptist, some say Elijah, and others say Jeremiah or one of the prophets.' "

As if Jesus would be impressed.

"But who do you say I am?" Jesus then asked his followers, to which Simon Peter replied: "You are the Messiah, the Son of the living God" (vv. 15–16).

Peter's response, if correct, carried significant implications. If Jesus indeed were the Messiah, then he was the one from the family of Abraham who would bring blessing to all the nations; he was the righteous Israelite who alone could keep the Law; and he was the Davidic king who could bring peace and justice to the world. And evidently he would do these things—bless the nations and fulfill the Law and realize lofty deliverables like justice and peace for all—through people just like Peter . . . those who believed in him and were devoted to him . . . the called-out ones . . . the church.

Peter's response indeed was correct, and upon the testimony that Peter had delivered, great things would soon unfold.

"You are blessed, Simon son of John," Jesus said to Peter, "because my Father in heaven has revealed this to you. You did not learn this from any human being. Now I say to you that you are Peter (which means 'rock'), and upon this rock I will build my church, and all the powers of hell will not conquer it" (vv. 17–18).

All indications are that Jesus meant what he said. Fifty days after the Passover, when he died and was buried and rose again, officially the church began. It was established on the bedrock truth that Peter had declared that day, that Jesus was the Messiah, the Son of God. And it grew, and grew, and grew. Some scholars, eager to know just how much and how fast it grew, have subjected the church's history to statistical analysis. Sociologist Rodney Stark was the first to take a real look at Christianity's track record, and in his book *The Rise of Christianity: A Sociologist Reconsiders History* he put forth some pretty staggering figures. Assuming a meager twenty believers as of AD 30 and a growth rate, on average, of 3 percent per year—a number he came to via a complex set of equations that I'll spare you just now—here is a sampling of where he arrived:

AD 30: 20 believers
AD 60: 1,280 believers
AD 100: 8,389 believers
AD 150: 36,000 believers
AD 200: 157,000 believers
AD 250: 676,000 believers
AD 300: 2,923,000 believers
AD 312: 3,857,000 believers
AD 400: 29,478,000 believers[1]

Yeah, I'd say that church got built. And since then the numbers have only grown. The *World Atlas*'s most recent assessment shows 2.2 of the world's 7 billion people identifying as Christians, making Christianity the largest religion in the world.[2] So the numbers, clearly, are impressive, but more impressive still is the *impact* the church has had. At its inception, the church prioritized the cooperative meeting of needs. In Acts 2:44–45, for example, we read that "all the believers met together in one place and shared everything they had. They sold their property and possessions and shared the money with those in need."

The church also prioritized caring for the sick and dying. Jesus healed the diseased during his earthly ministry; the early church advocated for medicine (alongside fervent prayer) in a culture that prized magic and superstition; and the first hospital, which was established at the end of the fourth century in Caesarea in Cappadocia, would lead to scores of building projects, all aimed at providing healing care.

There's the church's role in establishing orphanages, which was significant, and the church's role in feeding the hungry. The church has always stepped forward to support the widow, enfold the lonely in community, promote education for all people, welcome the stranger, rescue the suffering, drill the water well, pay the rent, buy the groceries, level the playing field, and stand up for rampant injustice wherever it is found. It is no stretch to say that no other group of people has had more significant impact on the world than *Christians*—Christ followers, the church.

As believers, when you and I think of the impact the church has had along the way, we are quick to rattle off the positive things, the contributions, the undeniable gains. But as those who prize truth, we must also acknowledge the negative impact the church has had. In the fourth century AD, Constantine legalized Christianity, which, despite his stated intent of protecting Christians from persecution, left believers subject to an awful and unwanted politicization of their faith. Five hundred years later, Holy Roman emperor Charlemagne's preferred form of evangelism was the ever congenial: "Convert, or die by the sword." Then came the two-hundred-year period of pope-sanctioned Crusades, and although the Catholic Church indeed increased in power and influence, the cost for that uptick was millions upon millions of lives. By any measure, the return on investment on that endeavor should never be seen as good.

The Spanish Inquisition and, later, the Salem Witch Trials were smaller or small in scope but still deplorable, and there was also the genocide of Native Americans, which was deplorable and *massive* in scale. In more modern times, the fringe operations acting on behalf of the church—the KKK, Westboro Baptist Church, groups who bomb abortion clinics, groups who would like to wipe the entire LGBTQ community off the face of the earth—have not done us any favors either.

I bring up these atrocities not to point fingers or throw stones. My purpose in bringing up the sordid parts of our history is to bring to light a question that any thinking person would ask: How is it that the same group of people can be responsible for the absolute best contributions to worldwide history while at the same time being responsible for some of the worst? Have you ever wondered that? The brother of Jesus, James, once said regarding the tongue that "sometimes it praises our Lord and Father, and sometimes it curses those who have been made in the image of God. And so blessing and cursing come pouring out of the same mouth. Surely, my brothers and sisters," James assessed, "this is not right!" (James 3:9–10).

How is it that the same group of people can be responsible for the absolute best contributions to worldwide history, while at the same time being responsible for some of the worst?

To further prove his point, James then provided a litany of seemingly ludicrous and rhetorical scenarios, saying, "Does a spring of water bubble out with both fresh water and bitter water? Does a fig tree produce olives, or a grapevine produce figs? No, and you can't draw fresh water from a salty spring" (James 3:11–12). And yet, to scrutinize the church's score card over the centuries of her existence is to find an outright estuary where both fresh water and salt water exist. The church helps and the church hurts: Haven't you found this to be true? We love the church and we see the brokenness in the church. Such a quandary we find ourselves in . . .

Complicating things further, I have found that that first question only leads to a second question, which is perhaps more important and relevant still: How can you and I ensure when history tells *our* generation's story, the tale of the church we were part of today, that we're on the good side of the ledger and not the bad?

I've been giving a lot of thought lately to that first question of how the very same group of people can be responsible for the best progress in society and also culpable for its digressions left and right. I've read books. I've engaged trusted pastors and scholars in conversation. I've studied Scripture. I've prayed. Further, I've tried to the best of my ability to weigh the temptations that I myself face. And what I've determined in my mind and in my heart and in my soul is that there are precious few reasons for the vast quantity of failures that we as the church have known. There aren't hundreds of reasons for the hundreds of wrongs done. There aren't scores of reasons or dozens of reasons or even tens of reasons why. In my estimation, whenever the church has gone off mission, leaving disillusionment and pain in her wake, one of but *three* clear reasons is to blame: lack of the Spirit's guidance, lack of integrity, or lack of love.

HYPE VERSUS THE HOLY SPIRIT

I was due to be in Texas for a ministry engagement years ago, and just before my trip a young man whose family I've known for years called and said he'd heard I was going to be in town and wondered if he could give me a ride to the event. He had a few questions he wanted to ask me, he said. I told him I'd love to talk.

This man was what I would consider a spiritual seeker, someone who isn't quite sure where he falls on the whole. Once in the car, the young man turned to me and said, "Pastor Brady, I don't want you to take this the wrong way . . . I want to trust you—and pastors in general. I've grown up in the church—you know that. But lately I've been having doubts. Whenever I go to church, I feel like I'm being 'sold.' I feel like I'm a fish on the line, and their goal is to reel me in. Everything is so *packaged*. Everything is so *produced*. Everything is so shiny and sparkly and *slick*. It leaves me wondering, *What are they trying to sell me? What trick do they have up their sleeve?*

"I don't want to feel this way," he said, "but I do. Just wondering what you think . . ."

The more this young man talked, the lower my heart sank in my chest. I've visited my fair share of slick churches; feeling "sold" is indeed the effect.

I think of Jesus' caution in Matthew 6 to believers regarding praying "to be seen by people" instead of praying to enjoy intimacy with God. So often along our faith journey, we must choose between the spectacle and the sacred. Around New Life, we liken the sacredness of our gatherings to a fire burning inside a fireplace. When Pam and I moved into our house, we had blowers installed on all the heaters so that when we turned on the gas fireplace in the living room, the entire house would be warmed. Now, we could also warm the house by simply piling up a bunch of firewood in the living room, striking a match, and standing back. But the unfortunate consequence there is that the entire house would burn down. Likewise, when we fail to "build the fireplace" in our gatherings—via those various structures and norms that Jesus himself asked us to prize—we can have a ball cheering for the wildfire in our midst, but we'll be standing among ashes in the end.

My counsel to churches in a marketer's day and age is to forgo the stunts and rely only on the Spirit. Put in the requisite structures so that the Holy Spirit can do his work. Quit overstimulating people's senses; steward their souls instead. Acts 2:43 promises that when the Holy Spirit is given free rein, a sense of *wonder* will unfold in your midst. We don't need to contrive the *wonder*ful; the wonderful already is in our midst.

HYPOCRISY VERSUS INTEGRITY

If I had to venture a guess, it would be that either you or someone you know has written off the entire institution known as "church" because of hypocrisy. "They're all hypocrites," the justification goes, "people who say one thing and do another." I've had numerous conversations with people who said those very words, and honestly, I couldn't blame them. In the eleven years I've been at New Life alone, I've watched more than a dozen high-profile pastors lose their ministries and their marriages after preaching kindness, goodness, self-sacrifice, and love from the pulpit while simultaneously either harboring deep sin or staying blind to their greed, gluttony, and/or tolerance for systemic oppression. "Hypocrisy" would be a generous way to put it. The fallout is always great. Compromise leads to a cover-up, which leads to cynicism once the truth comes out. Better to live according to our stated values. Better to be who we say that we are.

I love grace. I'm grateful for grace. I practice dispensing grace in day-to-day life. But if you are indulging a destructive lifestyle with no plans for doing an about-face, then a conversation is coming your way regarding God, his Word, and your heart. "I want you to be blessed," I'll tell you, "and that can't happen while you're choosing sin."

HERESY VERSUS LOVE

There is a third reasons the church gets off track, which is outright *heresy*, or teaching what's false.

When I was at Gateway Church, a young couple who was visiting our church for the first time approached me following the gathering and asked to talk with me for a few minutes. They were trying to decide if Gateway might be a good fit for them long term and wanted to run a few things by me toward that end. "Well, we don't exactly believe that Jesus was born of a virgin and that he was fully God," they began. "We think that when he was around thirty years old, he received a special call from God to be the Messiah, but we don't buy all of the virgin-birth stuff . . ."

There was a pregnant pause as I absorbed what they had just said.

"Is this going to be a problem?" they continued. "Meaning, will Gateway be cool with that?"

"Yes," I said slowly, doing my best to hide my shock. "To the first question, I mean . . . The answer to that one is yes. Yes, it will be a problem. No, it won't be cool."

Now it was their turn to be shocked. "You mean we can't keep coming to your church?" the husband said, his eyes wide, his frame tense.

"Of course you can keep coming to Gateway," I said sincerely. "You just can't lead in any way, shape, or form. The question of Jesus' divinity and humanity is not debatable in our house. You're messing with an absolute of our faith. . . . We believe the absolutes are absolute."

One of the first heresies that the local church had to deal with was pushback regarding the resurrection of Christ, and from that moment forward, false truths have spread far and wide. When the church wavers on the fundamental beliefs of our faith, that church will be led astray. This threat of diversion is what likely prompted the apostle Paul to write to his protégé Timothy about a time that was coming "when people will no longer listen to sound and wholesome teaching." He said, "They will follow their own desires and will look for teachers who will tell them whatever their itching ears want to hear" (2 Timothy 4:3). People will prize personal happiness over the pursuit of godliness and in effect will become their own popes. The advice here? *Run for your lives.*

In a scene from Matthew 16, we find Jesus being tested one day by the greatest religious leaders of the day, the Pharisees and the Sadducees, who demanded that Jesus show them a miraculous sign from heaven to prove his authority to them. In response and in the presence of his disciples, Jesus said, "You know the saying, 'Red sky at night means fair weather tomorrow; red sky in the morning means foul weather all day.' You know how to interpret the weather signs in the sky, but you don't know how to interpret the signs of the times! Only an evil, adulterous generation would demand a miraculous sign, but the only sign I will give them is the sign of the prophet Jonah" (Matthew 16:2–4), referring to the fact that just as Jonah had spent three days and three nights in the belly of a fish, Jesus would spend three days and three nights in the "belly" of our sin and the death that we deserve.

After that, Jesus left and went away.

Later, the text continues, after Jesus and his disciples crossed to the other side of the lake, the disciples discovered they had forgotten to bring any bread. "Watch out!" Jesus warned them. "Beware of the yeast of the Pharisees and Sadducees" (v. 6).

At this, "they [the disciples] began to argue with each other because they hadn't brought any bread. Jesus knew what they were saying, so he said, 'You have so little faith! Why are you arguing with each other about having no bread? Don't you understand even yet? Don't you remember the 5,000 I fed with five loaves, and the baskets of leftovers you picked up? Or the 4,000 I fed with seven loaves, and the large baskets of leftovers you picked up? Why can't you understand that I'm not talking about bread? So again I say, 'Beware of the yeast of the Pharisees and Sadducees'" (vv. 7–11).

Finally, the light came on: "Then at last they understood that he wasn't speaking about the yeast in bread, but about the deceptive teaching of the Pharisees and Sadducees" (v. 12).

I think about that scene from time to time, whenever I sense that as a church we're losing the plot. Of all the things we should be fighting for, right doctrine should top the list.

Admittedly, the church has gone astray in these three ways more times than anyone could count. The church has paid vastly more attention to scintillating theatrics than to sound doctrine, which has led the church to elevate charisma over character in their pastors and preachers and speakers, which has led to the church bending Scripture to declare things the Bible *simply does not say*. The apostle Paul, writing to his young protégé, Timothy, said to expect as much . . . and to remember with soberness of spirit the grave consequence of such a trend. "The Spirit clearly says that in later times some will abandon the faith and follow deceiving spirits and things taught by demons" 1 Timothy 4:1–2 (NIV) says. "Such teachings come through hypocritical liars, whose consciences have been seared as with a hot iron."

The abandonment of our faith . . . The unquestioning followership of "deceiving spirits" and "things taught by demons" . . . I don't know about you, but I want *nothing* to do with these things. And yet without love—genuine love, Spirit-empowered love, integrous love, this preeminent characteristic that is to be the hallmark of the Christian faith—we will undoubtedly deceive those we lead.

Diligence, then, is demanded, which is exactly what Paul exhorts: "Be diligent in these matters; give yourself wholly to them, so that everyone may see your progress. Watch your life and doctrine closely. Persevere in them, because if you do, you will save both yourself and your hearers" (1 Timothy 4:15-16, NIV).

Watch your life and your doctrine closely. Persevere in them, my friend. This thing called *church* . . . this mysterious, beautiful bride. For all its fractures and failures and missteps and junk, Jesus will never give up on her.

So, then, mustn't we.

We must believe in her and fight for her. We must preserve her and do our level best to present her faultless in the end.

A few years ago a friend of mine planted a church in Fort Collins, a progressive college town a two-hour drive north of Colorado Springs. Having spent time in Fort Collins, his heart was pulled toward the people, the culture, the spiritual need. In advance of his church's first service, he and several of his new staff walked the streets of Fort Collins in hopes of engaging people in conversation. The team wanted to know if there was a spiritual element to their story. They wanted to know if these people were part of a church and, if so, which one. The team wanted to know if the people they were talking to would be open to visiting this new church, what resources or opportunities they might find valuable, what depth of study might be helpful to them.

To my friend's surprise, in nearly every instance of talking with someone, the person said something to the effect of *Hey, I've got no issue with Jesus. Jesus is cool. I believe in Jesus. I like who the guy was. I just don't want anything to do with the church.*

"Why?" the team then asked. Nine times out of ten, the person being interviewed spoke of being "wronged" or "hurt" by the church.

They didn't hate the church, as it turned out. They just hated how the church had behaved.

I mentioned earlier the numerous conversations I've had along the way with people who are so fed up with the hypocrisy they see in "church people" that they have all but sworn off church. While the thought of being considered a hypocrite sends chills down my spine—I pray I'm never seen that way—I recognize the source of these people's frustrations, and I still don't lose hope. For the percentage of them who are willing to engage with me in deeper, earnest, and more candid conversation, the civil ground we always find is this: while they are indeed angry with the *way* that church has been done, they still believe in the *idea* of the church. It's a decent starting point; from there, real progress can be made.

As you might expect, the apostle Paul had input on this subject of persevering with the church for the believers gathered at Corinth, and to frame up his wealth of wisdom, I'd like to borrow some well-known words from Hebrews 10. On the heels of vivid exhortations to abandon the Old Testament approach to worship, which involved stringent rules, regular animal sacrifices, and the distinct feeling that enough was never enough—and to embrace Jesus as the "perfect sacrifice"—the writer offers a clear picture of where we've come from and where we can go from here. "The old system under the law of Moses was only a shadow," he wrote, "a dim preview of the good things to come, not the good things themselves. The sacrifices under that system were repeated again and again, year after year, but they were never able to provide perfect cleansing for those who came to worship. If they could have provided perfect cleansing, the sacrifices would have stopped, for the worshipers would have been purified once for all time, and their feelings of guilt would have disappeared" (Hebrews 10:1–2).

But then came the new covenant, and with it a new approach. "This is the new covenant I will make with my people on that day," God said. "I will put my laws in their hearts, and I will write them on their minds . . . I will never again remember their sins and lawless deeds" (vv. 16–17).

The writer then says, "And when sins have been forgiven, there is no need to offer any more sacrifices" (v. 18).

No more incense altars and high priests.

No more blood offerings and religious duties.

No more cleansing ceremonies and stone tablets.

Jesus was here now. And against that marvelous reality, we worship God in a whole new way. In verses 19 through 24, we find a picture of church as it's meant to be experienced. It's the church of our dreams, and yet this dream can come true. According to the last part of this passage, it's up to us:

If you want to stand out in the culture in which you find yourselves—if you want to be seen as truly remarkable—then *come together, encourage one another, and devote yourself fully to the cause of Christ.*

"Let us consider how we may spur one another on toward love and good deeds, not giving up meeting together, as some are in the habit of doing, but encouraging one another—and all the more as you see the Day approaching" (Hebrews 10:24–25, NIV). If you've ever ridden a horse, then you know that you can talk and command and *tsk, tsk* all you want, but there are times when the only thing that will make that horse trot is a little spur positioned in its thick side. A "spur" says, "Come on! Go! Get out of neutral here!" It's the exact image the writer of Hebrews longed to convey: *Let us come alongside other believers in accomplishing the mission of this thing called church.*

In so many words, Paul's three-pronged plea to the Corinthian believers is the same one I'd make to you today: If you want to stand out in the culture in which you find yourselves—if you want to be seen as truly remarkable—then *come together, encourage one another, and devote yourself fully to the cause of Christ.*

COME TOGETHER

The original Greek word for church, *ekklesia*, means the called-out ones, the ones who are bound as one unit, the ones who together are in the fight. The picture I carry in mind is that of a band of women and men and kids, arms locked and moving forward, while these discouraged ones linger back. Theirs is a lonely experience. It's an isolated experience. It's less than the life that Christ intends.

What Jesus intended, according to Acts 2, was that you and I and all who have put our trust in him as Savior would come together in his name, as modeled by the early church.

Daily, they met together in the temple courts. They gathered for the reading of Scripture and prayer. They praised God and enjoyed each other. They were one; they all belonged.

To the watching Greco-Roman world, this sight was amazing. Such diverse people were choosing fellowship with each other, and not anecdotally, but *over time*? What was the common denominator here? How were they getting along?

They had found their unity in Jesus. Jesus was their common bond. The church reveals to the watching world what's possible when Jesus is Lord over all.

DIVERSITY

It is far easier to gather with people who look like us, act like us, dress like us, vote like us, and spend their discretionary income on the same things you and I do. It's safer. It's less challenging. It's more affirming. And also: it's not church.

You may recall that the first recorded church-based scuffle happened between two groups of people, the Jews and the Greeks. "As the believers rapidly multiplied," Acts 6:1 says, "there were rumblings of discontent. The Greek-speaking believers complained about the Hebrew-speaking believers, saying that their widows were being discriminated against in the daily distribution of food." From that argument, a leadership structure was put in place so that responsibility for the overall group could be shared. Regardless of how noble our motivation or how progressive we are in our ways, human nature gravitates toward *likeness*, toward similarity, toward shared appearance and perspective and cause. This is hardly the way of Jesus, who said of the future: *all* knees would bend.

In Revelation 7:9, we see in John's vision a picture of a "vast crowd" gathering that is "too great to count" and that is made up of "every nation and tribe and people and language, standing in front of the throne and before the Lamb [Jesus Christ]." *Diversity*, not homogeneity, is what marks this gathering, a characteristic we can practice even now. When I look across our congregation at New Life on a Sunday morning, I take in a heartening sight. I see the guy in the Broncos jersey sitting two seats down from the transplanted Kansas City fan. I see the couple that just blasted our president on Facebook sitting across the aisle from the man who headed up Trump's local campaign. I see a man wildly devoted to the arts of tattoo and piercing a few rows in front of an ultraconservative homeschooling family of eight. I see a couple that hails from Africa and wears traditional African clothing each weekend mere seats away from a rough, tough Southerner who is trying to be healed of his racist ways.

And I think, *Now this* . . . this *is church*.

The rich need the poor, and the poor need the rich. The sick need the healthy, and the healthy need the sick. The young need the old, and the old need the young. The white need the black, and the black need the white. The conservative need the progressive, and the progressive need the conservative. The weak need the strong, and the strong need the weak. *All* of us need *all the rest* of us; it's how we learn and live and grow.

Yes, it makes things imperfect. Yes, it makes things messy. Yes, it makes things uncomfortable.

Yes, it makes it church.

CONTINUITY

In addition to diversity, we see in the early church great continuity. *Daily* those believers gathered together, and while that specific practice may be unreasonable in our modern day and age, the motivation behind it isn't, which is to *keep on showing up*.

Pam and I have been married for three decades and dated for two years prior to that, and in all that time we have been in church perhaps forty-nine or fifty Sundays per year. Regardless of where we are in the world, on Sunday we go to church. In addition to weekend services, if there is a Wednesday night prayer meeting, we go. If there is a Tuesday night Bible study, we go. If there is a Saturday morning volunteer opportunity, we go. Whatever's going on, *we go*.

I bring this up for a point of contrast. According to a recent Pew Research Center study,[3] roughly one-third of American Christians attend church each week, which means that roughly two-thirds are somewhere else.

Early followers *yearned* to come together, inconvenience and discomfort aside. They were *glad* when others said to them, "Let us go to the house of the Lord."

Think of it: the only reason we have the New Testament is because a group of sold-out believers was faithful to come to church. Every single story we have of Jesus happened in the context of the local church. Not one New Testament hero was *not* a member of a local church. Matthew, Mark, Luke, John, Paul, Timothy, and more—church members, every last one.

Most scholars agree that the New Testament was written between twenty and forty years after Jesus' death and resurrection, which means those stories had to survive somehow between when they occurred and when they were written about.[4] How did they survive? They survived by word of mouth. They survived by one person telling another person, *in the context of the local church*. They survived by believers gathering together to hear the tales one more time.

INTENTIONALITY

In addition to keeping the stories of Jesus' ministry and miracles alive, the early church prioritized certain practices that marked them as a group. They took communion, as Jesus had instructed them. They brought the tithe for the good of the poor. They studied the Scriptures and offered up heartfelt prayers. They baptized, and sang, and served. They came together to serve together. Which brings us to point number two.

ENCOURAGE ONE ANOTHER

The Greek word for "encourage" is *parakaleo,* a word that would have carried great meaning for Greek followers of Christ. In those days, when Greek military leaders lined up their armies for battle across a field, instead of sitting back watching the ensuing activity from a safe distance, they would actually join the fight. Members of the army were nervous, uncertain, and terrified of dying in battle, and so those leaders would come alongside those men with encouraging words: "I see you. I'm with you. I'm here. We're going to cross this field together. Borrow my strength until you have strength of your own. Victory will be sweet."

Invariably, those words would boost the armies' confidence, and victory indeed was sweet. It's a beautiful picture of church.

When we show up Sunday after Sunday, we encourage one another in the faith.

When ask a meaningful question, we encourage one another in the faith.

When we remember someone's name or circumstance, we encourage one another in the faith.

When we engage in worship wholeheartedly, we encourage one another in the faith.

When we say, "I see you . . . I'm here . . . I care," we encourage one another in the faith.

When we "put aside a portion of the money [we] have

earned" to be a blessing to others, as Paul said (1 Corinthians 16:2), we encourage one another in the faith.

But it is my contention that the *single greatest way* for us to encourage each other is by demonstrating our spiritual gifts. "A spiritual gift is given to each of us so we can help each other," the apostle Paul wrote in 1 Corinthians 12:7. It is by manifesting our distinct gifts that we pour courage in—*encourage*—when the world has drained all courage out.

It is impossible to read the whole of 1 Corinthians without picking up on the *maturity* theme. Paul spoke in chapter 2 of the fact that when he was among "mature believers" (v. 6), he could speak with wisdom, even as with the church at Corinth, he kept things "plain" (v. 4). He spoke in chapter 3 of needing to talk to those believers as spiritual "infants" who "belonged to this world" (v. 1). He acknowledged one verse later that they had yet to promote from "milk" to "solid food" (v. 2). He refers in chapter 4 to the Corinthians as his "children" (v. 14) and reminds them in chapter 14 not to be "childish" in their ways (v. 20). These references all beg the question: Well, then, how are we supposed to grow up?

In 1 Corinthians 12:8–10, the apostle offers a lengthy explanation of how *maturity in Christ* should look. It's like a well-functioning human body, Paul says: honorable, harmonious, in sync. "To one person the Spirit gives the ability to give wise advice; to another the same Spirit gives a message of special knowledge," he wrote. "The same Spirit gives great faith to another, and to someone else the one Spirit gives the gift of healing. He gives one person the power to perform miracles, and another the ability to prophesy. He gives someone else the ability to discern whether a message is from the Spirit of God or from another spirit. Still another person is given the ability to speak in unknown languages, while another is given the ability to interpret what is being said."

If you want to know how to encourage each other deeply, Paul essentially said, *be faithful to use your spiritual gift.* To play the role God has asked us to play is to mature in our spiritual walk. And what church doesn't benefit from mature believers? Maturity helps us all.

Throughout my ministry, I've seen the beauty and effectiveness of such a body working together, for God's glory and for its own good. I've seen *apostles* set things in order. I've seen *teachers* simplify complex subjects. I've seen *evangelists* share the good news. I've seen *prophets* speak the word of God. I've seen *pastors* rally around families in need. I've seen *leaders* bring reality from vision. I've seen those with *faith* heal the sick. I've seen the "harmony" that Paul speaks of in verse 25. I've seen that corporate *assistance* he says will show up. Which is how I know it's possible to fulfill the dream Paul claims can come true. When we come together not with the expectation of mere tolerance for each other but with that of truly *being with,* the natural by-product of that investment is genuine, unadulterated love, as we looked at in chapter 3. We become the people Jesus longs for us to be, gracious servants known for their love.

DEVOTE YOURSELF TO THE CHURCH OF CHRIST

A final word of encouragement. "Let us not neglect our meeting together . . . ," the author of Hebrews wrote. Let us "encourage one another" (Hebrews 10:25). And then this: *Let us not make this a fleeting occasion. Let us stay focused until Christ's return.*

As we looked at earlier, Jesus commissioned his followers before his ascension back to heaven with a task so huge, so widespread, and so impactful that it will indeed take us all to complete. We are to go into all the world and make disciples of all people, he said, baptizing them in the name of the Father, and of the Son, and of the Holy Spirit. So that's the job: Go, make, baptize. And he will be with us as we go.

I've always loved Peter's gentle encouragement along these lines. "You are a chosen people," he wrote in 1 Peter 2:9. "You are royal priests, a holy nation, God's very own possession. As a result, you can show others the goodness of God, for he called you out of the darkness into his wonderful light."

Isn't that a loving and gracious way to say: *Believers, get in the game*?

I tell our congregation that a big part of how I will ultimately define "success" at New Life is to have fewer and fewer "events." Fewer conferences. Fewer retreats. Fewer summer camps. Why? Because in the church of my dreams, we're all so occupied by serving the poor and enfolding widows in community and coming alongside families who have a parent who is deployed and reaching neighbors and praying their hearts out that we no longer need to be encouraged to go do those things. (And no longer depend on the government for such help.)

I long for a day when the local church is *so engaged in the fight to end human trafficking* that churches no longer need to hold awareness-building meetings to inform people about the victims' plight.

I long for a day when the local church is *so engaged in the work of bringing the gospel to people living far from God* that churches no longer need to schedule training sessions and organize mission trips.

I long for the day when the local church is *so engaged in loving well those in need in our neighborhoods and cities* that churches no longer need to craft elaborate strategies and outreach events for reaching out to those folks.

I long for us to be salt. I long for us to be light. I long for us to be *so devoted to our mission* that all other goals fade to gray. I long for us to be remarkable in our witness, and in our impact, and in our love.

Jesus gave his life for this body of believers.

He was compelled.

I pray we'd be too.

I was in Wales to meet with the remaining members of a dying Anglican church, to think and talk and pray about how to revive their once-strong and vibrant congregation. Between 2010 and 2012, half of churches in this country failed to add a single new member to their ranks, but the problem local churches are having is hardly an American one. The Welsh, too, are struggling to continue reaching younger constituents, this small church admittedly one of them.

After stepping out of my rental car, one of the priests escorted me along the cobblestone path to the church's entrance. As she and I walked, I couldn't help but notice that we were winding our way through a cemetery, the entire church surrounded by graves and tombs. *I can help explain your marketing problem,* I mused, even as I kept the thought to myself.

Upon entering the old building, I turned to the priest and said, "That was quite a graveyard . . . one of the largest I've seen. And right at the entrance to your church. Why is that, if I may ask?"

The priest's sober countenance brightened. "Oh!" She beamed. "Isn't that the *most* amazing thing?"

"I don't know," I said. "It seems a little . . . morbid . . . to me."

She physically took a step back. "No, no!" she said. "I'm afraid you're missing the point. In the three minutes it took us to arrive, you stepped past the tomb of my grandmother, who served the Lord for more than ninety years, and by the tombs of my great-grandfather and my great-grandmother, and by the tombs of my aunts and uncles and cousins, all of whom were fully devoted to the Lord Jesus until the day they died. They loved God in their generation and were known as being steadfast and strong. They prayed down the forces of hell when our country was under attack . . .

I long for us to be salt. I long for us to be light. I long for us to be *so devoted to our mission* that all other goals fade to gray. I long for us to be remarkable in our witness, and in our impact, and in our love.

"Every Sunday," she continued, "I have the honor and privilege of walking through their tombs to come to this place of worship, and every Sunday I am reminded of the great cloud of witnesses who urge me on."

> *Therefore, since we are surrounded by such a huge crowd of witnesses to the life of faith, let us strip off every weight that slows us down, especially the sin that so easily trips us up. And let us run with endurance the race God has set before us. We do this by keeping our eyes on Jesus, the champion who initiates and perfects our faith. Because of the joy awaiting him, he endured the cross, disregarding its shame. Now he is seated in the place of honor beside God's throne. Think of all the hostility he endured from sinful people; then you won't become weary and give up [Hebrews 12:1–3].*

"The church is like a river,"[5] New Testament scholar N. T. Wright once said. "Gradually other streams, other whole rivers, make their contribution.[6] They belong to each other and are meant to be part of the same powerful flow."[7]

In his closing address in his second of three letters to the Corinthian church, the apostle Paul gave the group but five goals to achieve. "Be on guard," he wrote. "Stand firm in the faith. Be courageous. Be strong. And do everything with love."

In other words: *Let the river flow.*

Let the remarkable river flow.

Acknowledgments

I'm so thankful for Pam, Abram, and Callie for giving me grace for this project. You are a remarkable family, and I love you very much.

I'm also thankful for the people of New Life Church, for their steadfast devotion and consistent witness. You are a most remarkable church.

Thanks also to Ashley Wiersma, who collaborated with me on the writing of this book. Your research, energy, and passion bring out the best in all of us.

Notes

Chapter 1: Corinth, U.S.A.—
What's in a Name

1. https://www.barna.com/research/half-churchgoers-not-heard-great-commission/.
2. Everett Ferguson, *Backgrounds of Early Christianity*, 3rd ed. (Grand Rapids, MI: Eerdmans, 1993), 70.
3. https://bible.org/seriespage/introduction-1-corinthians.
4. For more on the first-century cultural considerations that influenced Paul's ministry in Corinth, you might read Bruce W. Winter's *After Paul Left Corinth: The Influence of Secular Ethics and Social Change* (Grand Rapids, MI: Eerdmans, 2001).

Chapter 2: The Three Responses—
Believers in an Unbelieving World

1. On this subject of how believers engage an unbelieving world, H. Richard Niebuhr's is a classic one. For more, consider reading *Christ and Culture*, in which he lays out his five-part grid.
2. Malcolm Gladwell, *Outliers: The Story of Success* (Boston: Little, Brown, 2002), 167.

Chapter 3: The Fourth Way—
We Can Be a People of Remarkable Love

1. Everett Ferguson, *Backgrounds of Early Christianity*, 3rd ed. (Grand Rapids, MI: Eerdmans, 1993).
2. Bob Goff, *Everybody Always: Becoming Love in a World Full of Setbacks and Difficult People* (Nashville, TN: Nelson, 2018), 3.

3. https://www.goodreads.com/quotes/335-when-someone-shows-you-who-they-are-believe-them-the.
4. Joseph Parker, "Commentary on 1 Corinthians 8:4," in *The People's Bible* by Joseph Parker (1885–95). https://www.studylight.org/commentaries/jpb/1-corinthians-8.html1.

Chapter 4: Distinctly One—We Can Exhibit Remarkable Equality

1. https://www.thirteen.org/wnet/slavery/timeline/1776.html.
2. https://www.goodreads.com/quotes/631479-injustice-anywhere-is-a-threat-to-justice-everywhere-we-are.
3. https://kinginstitute.stanford.edu/encyclopedia/southern-christian-leadership-conference-sclc.
4. http://time.com/4927426/daca-dreamers-jeff-sessions-transcript/.
5. https://nwirp.org/Documents/Resources/DREAM/NWIRPDACA Checklist.pdf.
6. https://www.roadtostatus.com/top-5-benefits-of-daca/.
7. Christine Pohl, *Making Room: Recovering Hospitality as a Christian Tradition* (Grand Rapids, MI: Eerdmans, 1999), 166.
8. For audio of the event, access https://newlifechurchcs-my.sharepoint.com/:u:/g/personal/2018_nlcvideoarchive_newlifechurch_org/EbfMNCn_arJEgsxNcDAO-2oBu_hcbVkDEvz4ahon04Jcgg?e=e4mAKW; for video, https://newlifechurchcs-my.sharepoint.com/:v:/g/personal/2018_nlcvideoarchive_newlifechurch_org/Eda--fzdYHVLl8gJpDWY0OABxhOXNLUnmu7vS_yuxbstbw?e=JrzqyH.

Chapter 5: The Opposite of Condemnation—We Can Reflect Remarkable Grace

1. https://www.barna.com/research/a-new-generation-expresses-its-skepticism-and-frustration-with-christianity/.
2. https://en.wikipedia.org/wiki/Charleston_church_shooting.
3. https://www.washingtonpost.com/news/post-nation/wp/2015/06/19/hate-wont-win-the-powerful-words-delivered-to-dylann-roof-by-victims-relatives/?utm_term=.8c7cb365e572.
4. Keith and Kristyn Getty, "In Christ Alone." Getty Music, 2006.

5. https://www.newyorker.com/science/maria-konnikova/social-media-affect-math-dunbar-number-friendships.

Chapter 6: A Different Kind of Pleasure Pursuit—We Can Reflect Remarkable Sexuality

1. https://www.vanityfair.com/culture/2015/08/tinder-hook-up-culture-end-of-dating.
2. http://www.pewresearch.org/fact-tank/2016/02/29/5-facts-about-online-dating/.
3. https://www.covenanteyes.com/pornstats/.
4. https://www.huffingtonpost.com/2013/05/03/internet-porn-stats_n_3187682.html.
5. http://www.unh.edu/ccrc/pdf/CV169.pdf.
6. https://www.usatoday.com/story/news/nation/2014/08/19/hookup-marriage-weddings/14241739/.
7. https://www.psychologytoday.com/us/blog/strictly-casual/201401/in-hookups-alcohol-is-college-students-best-friend.
8. https://www.cdc.gov/std/life-stages-populations/adolescents-youngadults.htm.
9. https://www.lifesitenews.com/news/56-million-abortions-around-the-world-each-year-new-report.
10. https://www.vanityfair.com/culture/2015/08/tinder-hook-up-culture-end-of-dating.
11. Ibid.
12. Proverbs 5:3–4, 5–6, 7–8, 12–14, 15–17, 20–21, 22–23; 6:20–23; 7:4–5.
13. See Matthew 19:4–6.
14. https://www.nytimes.com/2017/11/10/arts/television/louis-ck-statement.html.

Chapter 7: To Say Yes, to Stand Firm, to Shine—We Can Build Remarkable Marriages

1. Timothy Keller, *The Meaning of Marriage: Facing the Complexities of Commitment with the Wisdom of God* (New York: Penguin, 2011), 28.

2. Ed Wheat and Gaye Wheat, *Intended for Pleasure: Sex Technique and Sexual Fulfillment in Christian Marriage* (Grand Rapids, MI: Revell, 1977), 39.
3. http://www.quotationspage.com/quote/1290.html.
4. Nancy Houston, *Love and Sex: A Christian Guide to Healthy Intimacy* (Washington, DC: Regnery Faith, 2018), 9.

Chapter 8: All of You, All the Time—
We Can Be Remarkable Worshippers of God

1. Jerry Bridges, *The Practice of Godliness* (Colorado Springs, CO: NavPress, 2016), 20.
2. See Matthew 14:28–31.

Chapter 9: Plugged In—
We Can Demonstrate Remarkable Power

1. https://www.inspirationalstories.com/quotes/cs-lewis-to-what-will-you-look-for-help/.
2. An interesting exchange on whether Gandhi actually said these words is found here: https://skeptics.stackexchange.com/questions/7973/did-mahatma-gandhi-say-i-like-your-christ-i-do-not-like-your-christians.

Chapter 10: A Foretaste of What's to Come—
We Can Hold Fast to Remarkable Hope

1. John Piper in an interview with *The Christian Post*: https://www.christianpost.com/news/john-piper-reflects-on-30-year-ministry-warns-pastors-to-avoid-stereotypes.html.
2. An entertaining article that explores this idea in the Arab world is found here: https://www.thenational.ae/arts-culture/ask-ali-why-it-is-rude-to-show-the-soles-of-your-feet-1.295633.
3. The Creed continues thus:

   We believe in one Lord, Jesus Christ, the only Son of God,
   Eternally begotten of the Father, God from God, Light from Light,
   True God from true God, begotten, not made, of one Being with the Father.

Through him all things were made.
For us and for our salvation he came down from heaven:
By the power of the Holy Spirit he became incarnate from the
 Virgin Mary
And was made man.
For our sake he was crucified under Pontius Pilate;
He suffered death and was buried.
On the third day he rose again in accordance with the Scriptures;
He ascended into heaven and is seated at the right hand of the
 Father.
He will come again in glory to judge the living and the dead,
And his kingdom will have no end.

We believe in the Holy Spirit, the Lord, the giver of life,
Who proceeds from the Father and the Son.
With the Father and the Son he is worshiped and glorified.
He has spoken through the Prophets.
We believe in one holy universal and apostolic Church.
We acknowledge one baptism for the forgiveness of sins.
We look for the resurrection of the dead,
And the life of the world to come. Amen.

4. For more on the ancient rabbinical Jewish view of this end-of-days resurrection, see Alfred Kolatch, *The Jewish Book of Why* (Middle Village, NY: Jonathan David, 1981).
5. See John 14:11.

Chapter 11: Let the River Flow—History Can Declare Us a Remarkable Church

1. Rodney Stark, *The Rise of Christianity: How the Obscure, Marginal Jesus Movement Became the Dominant Religious Force in the Western World in a Few Centuries* (San Francisco: HarperSanFrancisco, 1996).
2. https://www.worldatlas.com/articles/largest-religions-in-the-world.html.

3. http://www.pewresearch.org/fact-tank/2013/09/13/what-surveys-say-about-worship-attendance-and-why-some-stay-home/.
4. https://www.cru.org/us/en/train-and-grow/bible-studies/questions-about-the-new-testament.html.
5. N. T. Wright, *Simply Christian: Why Christianity Makes Sense* (New York: HarperCollins, 2006), 199.
6. Ibid.
7. Ibid, 200.